The Making of Equal Opportunities Policies in Universities

SRHE and Open University Press Imprint
General Editor: Heather Eggins

The Making of Equal Opportunities Policies in Universities

Sarah Neal

The Society for Research into Higher Education
& Open University Press

Published by SRHE and
Open University Press
Celtic Court
22 Ballmoor
Buckingham
MK18 1XW

and 1900 Frost Road, Suite 101
Bristol, PA 19007, USA

First published 1998

A catalogue record of this book is available from the British Library

ISBN 0 335 19808 2 (hb)   0 335 19807 4 (pb)

Library of Congress Cataloging-in-Publication Data

Neal, Sarah, 1966–
    The making of equal opportunities policies in universities / Sarah Neal.
        p.   cm.
    Includes bibliographical references and index.
    ISBN 0–335–19808–2 (hc). — ISBN 0–335–19807–4 (pbk.)
    1. Educational equalization—Great Britain—Case studies.
  2. Discrimination in higher education—Great Britain—Case studies.
  3. Minorities—Education (Higher)—Great Britain—Case studies.
  4. National Association of Teachers in Further and Higher Education.
  5. Association of University Teachers. I. Title.
  LC213.3.G7N43   1997
  379.2′6′0941—DC21   97–12934
                                                                        CIP

Typeset by Graphicraft Typesetters Limited, Hong Kong
Printed in Great Britain by St Edmundsbury Press Ltd, Bury St Edmunds, Suffolk

To Mum and Dad, to Su and Brock
With love

Contents

Acknowledgements

Many thanks are owed to both the individuals and organisations who made this book possible. Most obviously I want to thank the anonymous case study institutions, the AUT and NATFHE and all my research respondents for allowing me access and giving me the time and information which made the research project possible. I would also like to thank and acknowledge the Economic and Social Research Council which funded the research on which this book is based. I would like to thank my students and colleagues at Middlesex University for keeping me thinking and reminding me why equal opportunities in higher education is so important. Many thanks are due to John Solomos for all the invaluable guidance, advice and support over the last six years. Many thanks are due also to Barry Troyna, who always gave encouragement and insight. I am one among many who miss him. I owe countless thanks to Carol Vincent for her unfailing academic judgement and friendship, to Paul Connolly for tirelessly reading and advising on earlier versions of chapters and to Joanne Winning who is always there to share and dispel the doubts. The weaknesses in the book are mine alone and are unrelated to the supportive efforts of these people. I would like to thank Maureen Cox and John Skelton at Open University Press for their patience. Last, I would like to thank Su, who sees me through the hardest parts and makes everything easy.

Preface

Since 1945, the higher education system in Britain has increasingly occupied a more prominent position in society. The ascendancy of the notion of meritocracy, the Robbins Report, the creation of the local authority controlled polytechnics and the establishment of the Open University all contributed to higher education's shifting place in post-war British society. However, it has been the higher education policies of a successive Thatcher/Major Conservative administration that has most dramatically prised higher education from its seemingly remote location at the privileged peripheries of society and reset it more centrally. The Education Reform Act 1988 and the Further and Higher Education Act 1992 lie at the heart of the changed face of higher education in contemporary Britain. This legislation removed polytechnics and colleges of higher education from local authority control, ended the binary division between polytechnics and universities and, by allowing former public sector higher education institutions to apply for university status, created the 'new' universities. The restructuring of higher education has resulted in record numbers of people, including those groups traditionally excluded (black and minority ethnic[1] students, mature students, working-class students), entering (and gaining a) higher education.

The expansion of higher education not only coincided with the emergence of equal opportunities discourses and equal opportunities policies mainly in public sector institutions, but also in many private organizations and in the trade union movement (Lansley *et al.*, 1989; Cockburn, 1992). The higher education sector has not been immune from these developments, and since the late 1980s has increasingly engaged itself with the equal opportunities rubric. The arrival of equal opportunities on the higher education agenda can be seen partly as a reflection of the increasingly central social relocation of higher education, partly as a result of a growing student body, which included members of those groups not previously seen as natural constituents of higher education, and partly as an effect of the ascendancy of questions concerning social justice, particularly around the issues of race and gender. That equal opportunities concerns have arrived on the higher education agenda can be seen in such developments as the Committee of Vice-Chancellors and Principals *Codes of Practice on Equal Opportunities in Employment in Universities* (CVCP, 1991); in the establishment in 1993 of the Commission on University Career Opportunity (CUCO); in the creation in 1990 of the Higher Education Equal Opportunities Network; and in a proliferation of equal opportunities policies and structures in individual higher education institutions (*Equal Opportunities Review*, 1995). For example, in its 1993 survey of 106 universities, CUCO found that 93 per cent of the responding institutions had a formal equal opportunities policy, 79 per cent had anti-harassment policies and 72 per cent had guidelines on recruitment and selection (CUCO, 1994).

In some ways, it would be understandable to imagine that questions of equal opportunities would be sympathetically received in the higher education context. After all, higher education has long-standing traditional humanitarian and liberal associations. It has even had, due mainly to a brief period in the late 1960s and early 1970s, radical associations (Becher and Kogan, 1992). 'New middle class' theorists (Parkin, 1968; Gouldner, 1979) have identified higher education as a crucial site for the radical politicization of 'welfare professionals', and Halsey (1992: 236) asserts that the 'leftist tendency of academic professions in Western democracies is well known'. However, it would be a mistake to *assume* the receptiveness of higher education to equal opportunities issues. Higher education is a system which operates within (and generates) an intensely hierarchical, individualistic and competitive culture. Until relatively recently, higher education in Britain had mainly serviced a privileged minority and had had a role, albeit complex and often ambiguous, in furnishing the class and knowledge needs of the state in capitalist society (Tapper and Salter, 1978; Goldberg, 1993). Higher education also retains a heavy commitment to the notions of merit and meritocracy. For example, in their Commission for Racial Equality (CRE) funded survey of higher education institutions and equal opportunities policies (similar to CUCO's study but earlier and less optimistic), Williams *et al.* (1989: 24) found that 'Individual merit was seen as a neutral and non-negotiable attribute and discrimination or bias as unacceptable but unlikely to happen'.

That there is unease about higher education's engagement with equality issues is evident in the 'declining standards' debate which focuses on the ways in which an expanded and mass higher education system is detrimental to academic excellence (see, for example, Allington and O'Shaughnessy, 1992). This debate incorporates a sub-text which directly relates more (non-traditional students/new universities) with less (academic excellence). The concern here is not simply about how many, but more crucially, how many of *who*. Within these debates, equal opportunities policies are seen to have circumvented merit as a key access route into higher education and thereby contributed to the 'declining standards' of contemporary higher education (Williams *et al.*, 1989; Heward and Taylor, 1993).

The high profile staging and popularity of David Mamet's play *Oleanna*, in which the tension between a male professor and a female student who accuses him of rape culminating in his physical assault of her, serves as cultural indicator of higher education's unease as to the place of equal opportunities on its agendas. This unease can also be witnessed in the challenges that have been raised in relation to 'political correctness' in academia (hooks, 1989; Williams, 1992). Although these debates have occurred mainly in North American universities, they have fall-out for British universities in terms of a more general questioning as to the place of social justice discourses within the structures and operations of higher education institutions.

A somewhat extreme, but significant example of this was offered in a leader article in the *Daily Mail* (11 February 1994). Headlined 'Politically Correct! the Most Dangerous Two Words In The English Language Today',[2] John Patten, (the then) Education Secretary, claimed:

> What the PC thought police feed into young minds in schools and not so young minds in our universities, is that our society is by and large a conspiracy to do down 'minorities'. It thus tries to convince school children and the weak-headed (some students included, alas), that there is something fundamentally wrong with our values and way of life. In doing so it can brainwash our children into a resentful and suspicious view of us and our institutions, making them always on the lookout to protest, to complain, to demand. At its worst, it can make our young people strangers in their own land, with disastrous effects for all of us. *It is alien to everything British* (emphasis added).

It is no coincidence that in the 1990s attacks on 'political correctness' echo those made against equal opportunities (particularly anti-racism) in the 1980s. Despite the obvious idiocy of Patten's arguments, they clearly draw heavily on the staple new right anti-equality policy themes of subversion ('something fundamentally wrong with out values and way of life'), curbs on individual liberty ('brainwashing our children') and anti-Britishness ('strangers in their own land') (Gordon, 1990; Solomos, 1993).

Finally, it is worth noting that equal opportunities do not form any part of the Teaching Quality Assessment exercises, nor is equal opportunities an area that has been put forward for consideration by the Dearing Committee on higher education.

It is the contradictions that surround higher education that make it a particularly fascinating research site in terms of equal opportunities questions. While there has been some feminist commentary, on gender and higher education (Adams, 1983; Ramazanoglu, 1987, 1992; hooks, 1989; Williams, 1992; Henry, 1994; Leonard and Melina, 1994; Mirza, 1995; Nkweto Simmonds, 1997), until relatively recently higher education has tended to evade the research gaze in relation to race. It is as if 'racial discrimination is something to be studied in the world beyond the campus; it is rarely regarded as a real world issue within [the institution]' (*The Times Higher Education Supplement* 1983, quoted in Williams *et al.*, 1989: 8). However, events like the Commission for Racial Equality (CRE) investigation into the discriminatory admissions policy of St. George's Medical School (University of London) in 1988 (*The Guardian*, 25 February 1988; CRE, 1988), the industrial tribunal which found Leeds Metropolitan University guilty of race and sex discrimination for failing to appoint a black Asian lecturer in 1993 (Skellington, 1996), the findings of an Oxford University Students Union survey, which revealed that 97 per cent of black and minority students had experienced racism as verbal abuse or physical attack at the university (*The Times*, 8 December 1994), and the industrial tribunal which found Manchester University guilty on six counts of racial discrimination and victimization against a South Asian lecturer in the University's law department (*Observer*, 3 August 1997) all serve as public indicators that the issues of race and racism are very much present in higher education.

Within this context of ambiguity and contradiction, it is the ways in which higher education institutions have responded to equal opportunities issues, particularly race issues, that is the subject of this book. While there is a growing interest in the relationship between higher education and equal opportunities, the existing research and literature in the area remains embryonic. While the work, particularly of Farish *et al.* (1995) but also of Bird (1996), Heward and Taylor (1993) and Leicester (1993), offer qualitative insights, there is a quantitative bias to the majority of the research (Williams *et al.*, 1989; Jewson *et al.*, 1991, 1993; Modood, 1993b; CUCO, 1994; *Equal Opportunities Review*, 1995).

This book seeks to build on the existing literature by qualitatively exploring the response(s) of higher education to questions of equal opportunities in three ways. First, it analyses the character of equal opportunities policies, the processes of their formation and the structures put in place to implement these. Second, it focuses on the institutional discourses that surround equal opportunities policy in the everyday world of universities. Third, it is concerned with the ways in which the two main academic trade unions – the Association of University Teachers (AUT) and the National Association of Teachers in Further and Higher Education (NATFHE) – have been active, if at all, in raising and campaigning around equality issues. The role of academic trade unions in relation to equal opportunities in higher education is particularly important given the lack of attention paid to it in the existing higher education and equal opportunities literature.

Central to the book is an analysis of four university case studies conducted over an 18 month period between 1992 and 1993. The data from these case studies is drawn from two sources: the equal opportunities policy documents of each university and from a series of semi-structured interviews with various groups within these four higher education institutions – senior university management, staff whose brief includes a specific responsibility for equality issues, academics working in a related equality area and local academic trade union officials. The focus is on those responsible for equal opportunities policy generation and implementation, rather than on policy receivership and those groups whom the policies can affect (i.e. students).

The data is presented within a broader theoretical framework which considers such themes as the methodological dilemmas of researching race and equality questions in the higher education setting, the changing face of higher education, the political character and role of academic trade unions, and the contested nature of the equal opportunities discourse and the particularly problematic status of race within this. Chapter 1 is reflexively concerned with the actual research processes. It explores, through theoretical considerations and autobiographical experiences, the complementarity or otherwise of feminist and anti-racist methodologies in the research site. Chapters 2 and 3 set out the broader theoretical considerations behind the research. Chapter 2 explores the changing face of higher education in Britain and the relationship of these changes to equal opportunities questions. It concludes by providing a detailed profile of the four university case studies. The ambiguous and often contradictory ways in which the trade union movement has responded to equality questions is discussed in Chapter 3. Against this background, the chapter explores the histories and structures of the AUT and NATFHE and asks whether these unions and their members have/share values which are particularly sympathetic to equal opportunities politics. Chapters 4–6 are fieldwork-based. In part they are narrative, telling the story of the research findings, and in part they seek, by drawing on the arguments presented in the previous chapters, to explain the story. Chapter 4 analyses the textual content of the equal opportunities policy documents that were made available to me in the university case studies – what did these say and how did they say it? Using the interview data, Chapter 5 seeks to move behind the presentational data and explore what happens to equal opportunities policies and structures in the everyday world of the case-study universities. In particular, the chapter concentrates on why certain areas of the equal opportunities paradigm were 'comfortable' or 'easier' and which areas were 'uncomfortable' or 'difficult'. The position which the local AUT and NATFHE associations had taken up in relation to equal opportunities policy-making and policy implementation in the case-study universities is the focus of Chapter 6. It explores both the ways in which local trade union officials perceived their role in relation to equality concerns and the ways in which equal opportunities activists and senior management perceived the AUT and NATFHE in relation to equal opportunities. The book concludes in Chapter 7 by emphasizing the ambiguities and limitations of higher education's responses to equal opportunities issues.

1

Researching Equal Opportunities in Higher Education: Issues, Dilemmas and Self

Introduction

The (auto/biographical) experiences of conducting social research can be as significant as the actual findings of the research. This opening chapter is concerned with the relationship between the research project, the research process and the research self. Writing in the context of the United States, Stanfield (1993: xii) has argued:

> Social researchers who do study controversial social issues have been reluctant to come forward with autobiographical statements lest they be accused of promoting their own ideologies. Some feminists have been somewhat open in this area, explaining how their experiences as women have shaped their work, but as yet there have been no needed discussions by white feminists of how their class and ethnic origin have influenced their scholarship.

While higher education and academic trade unions may not immediately appear to present themselves as controversial research sites, the issues of race and gender are controversial, particularly when they are researched through anti-racist and feminist perspectives. From its conception, I identified my research project as anti-racist and feminist and identified the research process as being informed by anti-racist and feminist research methodologies. This chapter reflexively discusses the epistemological and methodological issues I encountered in attempting to negotiate the space between making these claims and the realities of conducting the research. This discussion centres on the relationship between the female/feminist researcher and her anti-racist research. The chapter argues that there is an inherent tension between adopting both a traditional feminist (reciprocal, egalitarian) approach and a traditional anti-racist (oppositional, challenging) approach. This difficulty raises a number of interconnected key questions:

What is the degree of compatability and comparability between anti-racist and feminist research? How transferable are anti-racist and feminist methodologies to a research site which has an upwards gaze directed towards the powerful? What qualifies (and disqualifies) research as anti-racist?

The chapter begins by tracing the rise of the anti-racist and feminist critiques of social research, charting their points of connection and their points of difference. Next, I outline the design of the research project and then offer accounts of my experiences in the field, researching equality issues in higher education.

Connecting and disconnecting race and gender: mapping anti-racist and feminist critiques of social research

While the anti-racist and feminist critiques of the dominant strands of social research appear on the surface to be well-suited allies, and have consequently often been placed, as in my own research, together, it is nevertheless crucially important that this apparently natural alliance does not obscure the diversities in the critiques' perspectives or their different histories. Perhaps the main linking point between the anti-racist and feminist critiques of social research, which both emerged predominantly in the early 1980s, is their shared notion that all research is political and involves issues of power and in their shared rejection of objective, apolitical, scientific research. Given this, Rex and Tomlinson's attack on radical black sociology for fusing politics and sociological analysis, and thereby detracting from the latter, can also be read as an attack on feminist sociology. When Rex and Tomlinson (1979: 314) argue that 'it is all too common today for sociologists to assert that their sociology is critical, non-value-free or reflexive and having done so to abandon any attempt to conform to the sorts of standards of reasoning and proof which are characteristic of scientific thought', they negate the evidence that these standards have been constructed according to a white, (and to a) male, canon.

The argument that all research is inherently political is not completely new. It can be traced to the critical theory tradition a decade previously which had questioned what the role and focus of social research should be, what criteria should be used to measure its validity and the relationship between social research and political struggles (Gouldner, 1971; Lukacs, 1971; Habermas, 1972; Mills, 1973).

In raising these questions, critical, feminist and anti-racist theorists have all highlighted the problematic direction of the social research gaze. In other words, much social research has tended to look downwards, leaning towards an interest in investigating those groups in society with marginal status, that is, the poor and the 'deviant' (Liazos, 1972; Gilroy, 1980). As Punch (1986: 25) notes, 'it is still painfully obvious that researchers have rarely penetrated to the territory of the powerful and many field studies still focus on lowly, marginal groups'. The downwards gaze tendency means that all too often the activities of the powerful evade investigation and patterns of oppression remain unchallenged. Goldberg (1993: 152) highlights the political significance of a social research agenda dominated by a downwards gaze when he argues that:

> social science furnishes the State and its functionaries with information, and it is often employed in formulating and assessing State policies to satisfy social needs. Ideologically the State often invokes expedient analyses and the results of social science, whether by collaboration or appropriation, to legitimise State pursuits and to rationalise established relations of power and domination.

Historically, research into the area of race has provided one of the primary examples of such a political and ideological role for social research. While this role may not be simply functional, 'it is disingenuous for . . . researchers to expect that their racist and patriarchal conceptualisations of black people will not be of interest to the state institutions which oppress black people' (Lawrence, 1981: 134). Within the context of research on race, or, more specifically, race relations, the gaze has not been on the 'state and its functionaries' but on black communities themselves. Social research on race not only lost sight of the issues of power and provided distorted and damaging presentations of black people's experiences and realities, it also offered a vehicle by which the collated data and information could be used to maintain and reinforce subordination and oppression (Bourne, 1980; Gilroy, 1980, 1987; Lawrence, 1981, 1982; Parmar, 1981; Gutzmore, 1983).

The anti-racist critique arose from the damaging and distorting (re)presentations of black people and the feeding of these into social policy-making and commonsense discourses. The anti-racist critique developed with the intention of conducting research that would aim to focus on how racism was reproduced and reinforced within different (white) social and state institutions and (white) cultural discourses. In making these arguments, the anti-racist critique can clearly be understood as a strategy for researching the powerful. Summarized (if crudely), the anti-racist critique (ibid.) represents a call to social research to shift its gaze from black communities and to investigate instead the 'white speaking' position.

It is significant that, historically, while black people have been constructed within social research agendas and via state-sponsored discourses as problematic and a potential threat to social cohesion and control, women[1] as a whole have tended to have been rendered invisible by social research and excluded from its agendas (Harding, 1987). In contrast to the anti-racist critique, the feminist critique arose therefore from the non-representation of women in social research. DuBois (1983: 107) argues that this invisibilization within the (mainstream) research process not only rendered women unknown but, crucially, also unknowable. For DuBois, it is the 'actual experience and language of women that is the central agenda for feminist social science and scholarship' (p. 108). Similarly, Duelli Klien (1983: 95) stated that it is only by having a 'methodology that allows for women studying women in an interactive process . . . that will end the exploitation of women as research objects'. Feminist methodologies developed around a commitment of doing non-hierarchical, reciprocal, emancipatory and subjective research which would be about women, for women and conducted from within women's perspectives (Oakley, 1981; DuBois, 1983; Duelli Klien, 1983; Stanley and Wise, 1983a, 1983b; Geiger, 1986; Harding, 1987). While I would endorse this project, it is possible to question whether feminist methodologies, located within these parameters, have offered any more than 'better' ways to research the powerless (i.e. women). As Smart (1984: 157) argued from her experiences of researching magistrates:

> in both Oakley's discussion on doing feminist research and in Stanley and Wise's book on the problems of research for feminists there is an assumption that the power imbalance between the people 'being researched' and the researcher is basically in favour of the latter . . . But my experience of researching the 'locally powerful' does not fit with this model at all . . . I find this assertion remarkable and only explicable if we ignore all social class divisions and the structures of dominance in society outside the academic world of research.

With more recent developments, feminist methodologies have moved away from simply 'inserting' or making gender more visible to a focus on issues of power in the context of gender as a social division and to a theorizing of women's experiences of gendered power relations (Currie and Kazi, 1987; Gelsthorpe, 1992; Opie, 1992; Ramazanoglu, 1992). However, these developments cannot be read as a call to research the 'male speaking' position in the same way that the anti-racist critique clearly demanded that racism should be researched through the investigation of the 'white speaking' position. Given this gap in terms of the comparability of the two critiques, their *compatibility* becomes problematic for the researcher who is attempting to apply both critiques to their research process. While I will explore the tensions in reconciling anti-racist and feminist approaches in the actual research field, it is the development and design of the research that I wish now to discuss.

Developing and designing a research problem through anti-racist and feminist perspectives

I intended my own research to be a project that would address the issues of equal opportunities and anti-racism through inquiry into (predominantly) *white* institutions. These institutions consisted of four case-study universities – two 'old' universities and two 'new' universities – and two academic trade unions, the AUT and NATFHE. The focus on universities and academic trade unions as white-led institutions was directly linked to the anti-racist demand that it is the ways in which racism is reproduced and reinforced within social and state institutions which requires research attention (Bourne, 1980). However, having a research focus on white institutions is not without complexities. As Back and Solomos (1992: 13) note in relation to their own research:

> for researchers to speak rhetorically about their mission to study white racism and institutions contains a subtle slight of hand. While superficially this seems more credible other important issues emerge. On one occasion Les Back offered an account of our 'studying the speaking position of the powerful' to a long established black activist. He reminded Les that to do so would be comparable to studying slavery by only speaking to the slave masters. It was within this kind of context that the rhetoric of our position broke down.

While recognizing that the case-study universities were not exclusively white, I decided that I would only approach black university staff if they fell into my relevant respondent groups. I needed to include black participants so that I could hear black perspectives, but I did not want to include black participants simply because they were black. I did not want to collude with the common assumption that blackness is synonymous with expertise in the area of equality in general and race in particular. As one black respondent commented to me, 'because you're black it's assumed you've been out on the streets all your life fighting the National Front'. The 'experts' theme was one that continually surfaced in the field. A full and detailed breakdown of my sample, according to gender, ethnicity and occupational status, is contained in Tables A1–A3 in the Appendix.

At its most basic level, the validity of my claims for conducting anti-racist and feminist research rested on my commitment to 'problematizing' the issues of race (and gender) within the institutions being investigated. Building on this, I legitimized the anti-racist/feminist identification of the research in terms of its ability to make sense of the origins and nature of racist and sexist practices and discourses, and its ability to effectively critique countering (i.e. equal opportunities, anti-racist) practices and discourses (Connolly, 1993). This may appear a rather fragile foundation given that the wider context of what actually qualifies as anti-racist and/or feminist research is often judged according to more tangible criteria; for example, the ability of the research to contribute towards specific anti-racist and/or feminist struggles, most obviously through collaborative action research (Oakley, 1981; Ben-Tovim *et al.*, 1986; Lather, 1986; Troyna and Carrington, 1989; W. Ball, 1991, 1992). While these writers have argued that it is collaborative action research which sits most comfortably with anti-racist and/or feminist commitments, such a methodology only seems fully appropriate to those research sites which are concerned with powerless groups and in which the researcher inhabits a powerful position.

The research was qualitatively designed. This was because of the need for more qualitative insight into the complex, micro politics of the everyday world of higher education institutions (Farish *et al.*, 1995) and because of the quantitative bias of the existing higher education and equal opportunities research (Williams *et al.*, 1989; Jewson *et al.*, 1991, 1993; CUCO, 1994). This decision was made not simply because of the association of qualitative research with anti-racist and feminist methodologies. While quantitative and qualitative research are essentially neutral, it is the way in which each has specifically been employed that has rendered them objective/scientific/masculine/feminist/anti-racist (Gelsthorpe, 1992) and, as Morgan (1981: 86–7) has noted, qualitative research has its 'own brand of machismo with its image of the male sociologist bringing back news from the fringes of society, the lower depths, the mean streets'.

Although case studies have received some criticism (Hammersley, 1992a), using case-study methods allows for researching complex social institutions like universities and complex issues like equal opportunities, making it possible to gather the perceptions, beliefs and actions of a variety of participants in a variety of positions within an institution (May, 1993). The value of the data collected through case studies lies in the richness and degree of insight that micro-level research is able to offer in terms of understanding macro structures (Ball, 1987). I used four university case studies to examine in what ways higher education had responded to equal opportunities issues and to examine how these responses were generated, how they operated and how they were received in the complex, everyday world of higher education institutions. Detailed profiles of the four university case studies are contained in Chapter 2 and detailed profiles of the AUT and NATFHE are provided in Chapter 3.

Within the case studies, I used two main sources for data collection. The first source of research material arose through my collection of various equal opportunities policy texts and documentation that was made available to me in each case study and by the AUT and NATFHE. The second and primary source of data came through the 91 semi-structured, one-hour interviews I conducted with a number of target respondent groups. As noted earlier, these respondent groups consisted of senior university management, trade union officials, members of university staff who had a formal/specialist responsibility for equal opportunities, and members of staff who were informally interested and/or involved with equal opportunities. Although I recognized differential degrees of power among individual respondents within these target groups, I categorized them overall as powerful in terms of their professional status. The main themes that the interviews sought to explore with respondents centred around the interpretations of the concepts of equal opportunities and anti-racism; the appreciative context of equality policies – what aspects of these policies were contested (why, in what ways and by whom); and what aspects of these policies were supported (why, in what ways and by whom); and the role and relationship of academic trade unions to equality policy formations and implementation (a full interview schedule is given in Table A4 in the Appendix). The findings of the research are the subject of Chapters 4, 5 and 6 (see also Neal, 1995a).

What I now explore are the political and ethical dilemmas I encountered as I attempted to accommodate my anti-racist, feminist rhetoric with the research process itself.

In the field – experiences of power and powerlessness

Doing anti-racist research: the confrontational feminist researcher?

Since the mid- to late 1980s, the period when anti-racism 'irrevocably stumbled' (Hesse *et al.*, 1992: xvii), a number of commentators on the left (Gilroy, 1987, 1990; Macdonald *et al.*, 1989; Nanton and Fitzgerald, 1990; Hall, 1992; Modood, 1992; Rattansi, 1992; Brah, 1993; Goldberg, 1993; Gillborn, 1995) have been concerned with analysing the relative failure of anti-racism as a concept and as a policy. This concern has focused not on opposition from the right, but on the inadequacies of the anti-racist discourse itself and the possible futures for it. Much of this debate has drawn on post-modernist discourses and in doing so has criticized the essentialist black/white dichotomy of anti-racism. This debate has sought instead to theorize the complexities of the interplay between race, ethnicity, culture, gender and class and highlight the notion of 'hybrid identities'. As Hall (1992: 254) has noted: 'What is at issue here is the recognition of the extraordinary diversity of subjective positions, social experiences and cultural identities which compose the category "black"'.

Similarly, Brah (1993) has argued for the recognition of a '*multiplicity* of ideological, cultural and structural factors' (p. 456, emphasis added) and emphasizes the 'intersections between gender, class, ethnicity, racism, religion and other axes of differentation' (p. 441). In the cogent critique of anti-racism offered by Gilroy (1987, 1990), he has argued against 'statist conception(s)' in which the local state is seen as the 'main vehicle for advancing anti-racism'. This statism has 'actively confused and confounded the black community's capacity for autonomous self-organisation' (Gilroy, 1990: 208). For Gilroy, the first key deficiency of anti-racism has been its inability to counter the New Right discourses around race which actually appear not to be about race: 'Anti-racism has been unable to deal with the new forms in which racism has developed. In particular, it has been incapable of showing how British cultural nationalism becomes a language of race' (p. 200). The second key deficiency has been the inherent reductionism of anti-racism – that is, its universalistic presentation of white people as the problem and black people as the victims. This has been the basis for the 'disastrous way' in which anti-racism has 'trivialised the rich complexity of black life by reducing it to nothing more than a response to racism' (p. 208). It has been this trivialization which has resulted in the reification (and romanticization) of certain aspects of black life (hooks, 1982; Anthias and Yuval-Davis, 1992).

For Gilroy, there is a contemporary need to go beyond anti-racism and to develop a plurality in both the concept and the associated policy strategies of anti-racism. It has been the very singularity of anti-racism which has contributed to its reductionism and its reification of race. The emphasis on plurality is an essential aspect in any revision of anti-racism. Given this emphasis on plurality, modes of resisting racism(s) have to be able to take into account the multidimensional aspects of oppression if they are to have any measure of success. Gilroy (1990: 208–9) has noted that 'there can be no single or homogeneous strategy against racism because racism itself is never homogeneous'. Similarly, Goldberg (1993: 213) has stated, 'racism's adaptive resilience entails that we have to respond with sets of oppositions that are found in and through praxis to be appropriate to each form racism assumes'.

However, what is not always clear in the demands to move beyond essentialist anti-racism is what policies, constructed within such a framework, would actually look like (Gillborn, 1995). As Gilroy (1990: 72) argues 'at a theoretical level "race" needs to be viewed much more contingently, as a precarious discursive construction', although 'this does not of course, imply that it is any less real or effective politically'. This is an important point because, given the extent of the leftist critique of anti-racism, the critique can seem to represent a demand for the end of anti-racism. This was illustrated by the events surrounding the publication of the Macdonald Report (see Gillborn, 1995). The critical position that the Macdonald Report took in relation to the anti-racist policies in Burnage High School was cited by the right as evidence of the dangers of anti-racism. However, the authors, while rejecting the old essentialist model of anti-racism, strongly asserted their support for strategies which sought to 'confront' racism (Macdonald *et al.*, 1989: xxiii–xxiv). Yet it is difficult to see how a new model of anti-racism, which retains its confrontational elements, can secure itself a place on the type of acceptable (depoliticized) equality agenda which organizations are willing to take up in the 1990s (see Chapter 5). What is clear is that today, anti-racism as both a concept and an anti-oppressive strategy inhabits a complex and hazardous terrain as it negotiates and re-shapes itself between the leftist rejection of its former reductionist black/white dichotomy and the successful New Right anti-anti-racist attack. What is also clear is that in these revisionist processes, an anti-essentialist version of anti-racism retains the notions of dissent and challenge at its heart (see, for example, Macdonald *et al.*, 1989: xxiii–xxiv). As I have argued elsewhere (Neal, 1995a; Chapter 4), the term (and concept) of anti-racism continues to have oppositional and confrontational rather than harmonious and consensual connotations. While having the former associations has contributed towards the populist perception of anti-racism as extremism (Ben-Tovim *et al.*, 1992), they have also imbued anti-racism with a particular masculinity. The female/feminist researcher faces then certain difficulties in adopting a masculinist (objecting/dissenting/challenging) approach in her research. Women do not tend to easily or confidently inhabit this masculinist terrain. Despite the extent to which she is/may be committed to the anti-racist project, being objecting/dissenting/challenging and thereby anti-racist can involve a complex internal struggle with (her)self. Similarly, feminist research methodology does not always comfortably accommodate a challenging dimension and this can involve the feminist researcher in a complex external struggle with her research process. It is to my own negotiations of these struggles that I now turn.

I had not been in the field long before I recognized that the interview technique can become problematic when researching 'sensitive' issues like race, in that it provides very little space for dissent or objection on the part of the researcher to what a respondent may be saying. Although feminist standpoint research has been widely criticized for being essentialist, unrealistic and restricting, the flip side of symmetrical researching – white people interviewing white people about race and racism – carries as many complexities. Most obviously, such symmetry may entail the presumption that the researcher and the respondent, through their shared whiteness, will share the same (racist) views and ideas. While I did encounter this on occasions, more often I experienced white respondents interpreting this (symmetrical) research situation as a 'safe zone'. The most obvious indicators of this was a regularly professed 'fear' of 'saying the wrong thing' and not being sure of the 'right' language to use when discussing race issues. Such confessions were couched in terms of a well-meaning innocence or confusion, but they also reflected both an inability on the part of white people to constructively 'talk race' and a deeper white fear of black people (hooks, 1996). For example, this excerpt comes from an interview with the women's unit co-ordinator in one of the 'new' university case studies:

WUC: With gender people are relatively happy about what the issues are and what needs to be done, but with race it's foggy, it's not often talked about and people feel unsure about what we should be doing, what language to use. They don't want to look like idiots and they don't want to offend anyone.

SN: Why do you think talking about race is so difficult?

WUC: Well for the reasons I've just said I suppose, not being certain of the issues and being scared of being called racist . . . race is a tricky area.

Echoing these 'fear/uncertainty' themes, at the end of an interview with the chair of the race advisory committee in the same case study, he (a white man) asked me if I would comment, not on what I thought of the university's initiatives around racial equality or the work of the committee, but on the language he had used to discuss race in the interview. Collapsing race into a language dilemma (for white people) serves to relegate race to a marginalized category which prevents race issues being discussed or acted around in any meaningful way.

Both these situations raised questions as to how a white researcher, researching race from a professed anti-racist position, should respond to racist discourses and the confessed language 'fear' encountered in the interview process. How does a researcher in this position offer objections or challenges to racism without jeopardizing the interview and, perhaps, if the respondent is powerful, access to the whole case study. Even if the outcome is not so extreme, an objection could result in a significant alteration in the nature of what the respondent is prepared to tell the researcher. Similarly, in what ways, if at all, should the researcher enter into a 'what is the right' language debate? Yet to remain silent implicitly implies either consent (Back and Solomos, 1992; Keith, 1992; Solomos and Back, 1995); or a shared uncertainty as to the 'right thing to say'.

My non-committal probing of respondents meant that I encountered an uncomfortable gap between my self-definition as a anti-racist political activist prioritizing the need to challenge racism in the variety of sites in which it emerges and being an academic researcher. When I did remain silent when racism or problematic language use was encountered in the interview process, my political dilemma was acute. That I had 'sold out', colluded and compromised were feelings that I continually dragged along with me through the fieldwork.

The nature of who I was researching and to some extent what I was researching meant that when I did encounter racism it was often couched in the terms of the new racism. In one particular incident, I had been interviewing a pro-vice-chancellor. Throughout the interview he had been cooperative and friendly and had spoken repeatedly of his commitment to equal opportunities in the university. After the interview, he showed me to his office door and commented on the complexity of the area I was researching. I was vaguely agreeing (as I was walking) when he started talking about 'difficulties between cultures'. Standing in his office doorway he told me:

> we've had difficulties in the library for example. We have Asian students who are quiet and want to work hard and they get upset when the silence in the library gets disrupted by Afro-Caribbean [*sic*] students. They [Asian students] don't understand that it's their [African-Caribbean students] nature to be happy and exuberant.

At first, I thought he was saying that these attitudes were common in the university and that they needed to be addressed, but then I quickly realized he was giving me anecdotal evidence of his own theory that it is (biological) culture that leads to misunderstanding and racialized problems and conflicts. When I did realize this, my first reaction was not to challenge this notion but memorize what he had said in order that I could go and record it accurately. My choice to act as an 'objective' and apolitical researcher immediately raised political and ethical dilemmas. As W. Ball (1990: 17) has argued, 'the fusing of the role of researcher and political activist are difficult to reconcile with the expectations of the academic world, with its emphasis on individual achievement, objectivity and academic publication'. Other commentators engaged in researching race have noted similar experiences. Back and Solomos (1992) write of being 'haunted' by the dilemmas surrounding these issues. In relation to his own research, Keith (1992: 554) writes of 'sitting in an area car in one of the police divisions of the Metropolitan Police notorious for confrontation between police and the black community' and spending 'eight hours giving tacit approval to the policing judgements of the two officers in the car by my own failure to challenge several comments that I had found offensive'.

While not intending to detract from the experiences of these researchers, it is necessary also to understand the dilemma in the context of gendered power relations. I came increasingly to interpret this situation within a gendered framework. As I argued earlier, there is an inherent masculinity in the confrontational or oppositional associations of anti-racism. When Lynn Barber ironically and incredibly argues that 'women are better at interviewing men, possibly because they are more experienced in listening and they don't feel obliged to correct or criticise or argue' (*The Guardian*, 14 February 1994), she is actually nearer to identifying a reality than the first reading of the quote indicates – that is, if 'obliged' were to be replaced by 'expected'. This is to return to my earlier point regarding the constraints of research methodologies and the essentially passive and facilitating role of the interviewer. A anti-racist researcher may feel the political need to counter racism in the research process whether they are male or female and equally face the dilemma of how actually to do this. However, given the associations of women with facilitating speech and listening, such a challenge becomes additionally difficult in that it would also challenge the conventionally perceived role and behaviour of women. For a feminist researcher who remains silent on her encounter with racism, she implies her complicity with this racism *and* she conforms to the expectations of the 'typical model of male/female verbal exchange' (Smart, 1984: 156). It is to the gendered experience of the research process that I now turn.

Doing anti-racist research: struggling and colluding with the feminine self

In perhaps his most legitimate criticism of feminist methodology and the issue of hierarchy, Hammersley (1992b: 196) noted that:

> where men are included as sources of data, hierarchy cannot or should not be eliminated from the research process. The men may impose a hierarchy and, whether they do or not, presumably feminist researchers must exploit whatever resources they have to exert control over the relationship, on the grounds that in present circumstances the only choice is between being dominant or being dominated.

Hammersley's argument has direct relevance to my research process for a number of reasons: that I was regularly interviewing (powerful) men; that

I was asking questions about issues which are perceived as controversial; and that I was a young, female researcher. The combination of these factors pushed me to a position in which my fieldwork constituted a specific site for my own domination and marginality against which I had constantly to struggle.

My awareness of my marginality was reinforced by the environment in which the interviews were conducted, overwhelmingly in the respondents' own offices, a spatial symbol of professionalism. When interviewing senior management respondents, I would have to announce my arrival for an arranged interview to a secretary or personal assistant. An interview would often be interrupted by seemingly urgent telephone calls or a secretary or personal assistant coming in and reminding the respondent that they had a meeting to go to directly after their interview with me. If I was offered coffee, it was ordered for and bought in by the secretary or personal assistant. This intimidating milieu intensified the experience of interviewing powerful people. Before such an interview, I would be acutely anxious and would check my tape recorder many times to make sure it was set up correctly and check my interview schedule simply to make sure I had it to hand. The simple routines of doing these tasks became infused with the need to appear smoothly professional and capable, to fit into the environment. Discovering that the tape was in the wrong way round and having to search through my bag to find my interview schedule in front of the respondent were trivial situations that I dreaded happening. Being offered (the served) coffee, which I always felt I should accept, not only made me uncomfortably aware that it was made and brought to me by a (female) secretary, but it also presented particular ordeals simply in terms of drinking it at the right intervals and not spilling it. When interviewing one vice-chancellor in a midday slot, he ordered that lunch should be brought up to his office for both of us. Negotiating eating the food, asking the interview questions and presenting myself as a professional was especially difficult. It is hard to convey these anxieties – they appear almost comical now and can be explained in part by my inexperience. They can also clearly be interpreted in the gendered context of my marginality (Finch, 1984; Wilkins, 1993).

In responding to this marginality, I increasingly reverted to an uneasy and ironic adoption of a traditional, 'malestream' academic persona, presenting myself as neutral, rational and objective as an attempt to claim an authority which I felt necessary to conduct interviews with respondents. Hammersley (1992b) argues that there is nothing intrinsically wrong with the researcher exercising control over the research process and that, unavoidably, the researcher, simply by engaging in the research process, is making a claim to intellectual authority of some form. However, trying to take on the guise of the objective academic engaged in neutral research was problematic not only because of the political and ethical compromises I was making, but also because women are not perceived as being able to be neutral and objective or as having intellectual authority. This had repercussions in terms of how I began to think of my physical appearance. I not only had to (pretend to) be objective, I had to *look* as if I were objective. This requirement rendered bright red lipstick, birds-nest hair, torn Levis and eight-hole Doc Marten boots unwearable. Measor (1985: 62) recommends that when interviewing (presumably only when you are a woman), 'it is very important to come over as very sweet and trustworthy, but ultimately rather bland'. Conforming to this gendered stereotype, I replaced what I would normally wear with an innocuous or neutral dress code. In a different context – that of lesbian fashion – Blackman and Perry (1990: 74) make a relevant point when they refer to such a process as the presentation of the 'blank page': 'it is difficult to read into this fashion any indication of sexual politics or practice, and it will not always be clear whether the wearer is a lesbian'.

Although dress and appearance have been the subject of some feminist discussion (Wilson, 1985; Blackman and Perry, 1990), given the emphasis that feminist methodologies have had on women interviewing women, it is not surprising that very little has been written from a feminist perspective about how women dress when they are in the field. Those feminist researchers who have written accounts of how they dressed during their fieldwork were, significantly, conducting research on men. Carol Smart (1984: 153) indicates this dilemma about how to appear:

> one important element was how the researcher presented herself and a vital element of that was dress . . . in my research there were several pitfalls to avoid. One was dressing too casual as minor officials in particular would tend to disbelieve I was a bona fide researcher. It was difficult to gauge whether to try and look like a probation officer, a solicitor, or a stereotyped woman academic.

Although in many ways dress and appearance may seem a minor or trivial aspect of the fieldwork process, it is actually an important part of all ethnographic research. In their research into street homelessness in Austin, Texas, Snow and Anderson (1993) write of how they 'dressed down' to fit more easily into the environment of front-line homelessness. Yet for women, dress and appearance are closely linked to a variety of sexual sub-texts in ways that they are not for men.

My own dilemmas about what to wear were very much to the fore of my thinking when I was going to interview a man in an overtly powerful position. Even when I did interview women who were in senior positions, my anxieties over my physical appearance were much less intense. This would indicate the proximity of the context of (hetero)sexuality and interviewing men (see, for example, McKee and O'Brien, 1983).

The account offered by Gewirtz and Ozga (1993) of their experiences of doing lifestory interviews with 'elites in educational policy making' raises connected issues of sexuality in the interviewing process, most significantly the notion of collusion with the (hetero)sexual sub-texts. Gewirtz and Ozga (1993: 1) note that as their research progressed:

we were obliged to acknowledge . . . that the fact we were both women eased our access to our almost exclusively male interviewees. That in itself, of course raises ethical issues, which are heightened when we acknowledged that our non-threatening and sympathetic self-presentation was also a useful research tactic.

Later in their paper, Gewirtz and Ozga (1993: 12) take up this theme again, stating:

in effect we felt that we were viewed as women in very stereotypical ways . . . and we were obliged to collude to a certain degree, with that version of ourselves because it was productive for the project. *We were given a great deal of help by our interviewees and they told us a great deal about themselves* (emphasis added).

Clearly, this successful means of collecting data was significantly enhanced by the collusion of these women researchers and their manipulation of their marginality.

The collusion of women interviewers with the (hetero)sexual sub-text which Gewirtz and Ozga highlight, and which my own adoption of a 'Miss Marks and Spencer look' also represents to a certain extent, has similarly arisen in a media context. For example, Anne Leslie of the *Daily Mail* advises that 'it is best to be neat but not gaudy; to be attractive but not so much that you have *Playboy* phoning up', and Nina Myskow of *The Sun* baldly asks, 'isn't every interview a seduction?' (*The Guardian*, 14 February 1994). Although such comments may be problematic, they echo the same dilemmas as expressed by Smart (1984), McKee and O'Brien (1983), Gewirtz and Ozga (1993) and myself.

The interview, then, can compound both the (hetero)sexual sub-text and the traditional role of women as listeners. As Lynn Barber of the *The Sunday Times* notes, 'listening with rapt attention is far more seductive than a mile of cleavage' (*The Guardian*, 14 February 1994). Listening is essentially a feminized occupation and women are often structurally located in, and informally coerced into, positions of encouraging and facilitating male speech (Spender, 1980; Smart, 1984). This process is being reproduced directly when women interview powerful men, irrespective of whether or not they are feminists or informed by feminism.

Doing anti-racist research: experiencing hostility

My neutralized appearance and my attempts to present myself as objective were undermined to a large extent by what I was actually researching. As a young, low-status, woman researcher, I represented very little threat to the powerful people I was interviewing (and I had gone some way to presenting myself as non-threatening), yet I still met with some hostility which can most accurately be understood in terms of the issues I was investigating. This hostility was not usually overt but tended to be expressed in a variety of ways that spilled over into my marginality and my gender. I would often be kept waiting for an interview, long after the arranged time. To be treated patronizingly, with seeming indifference or with the respondent continually looking at their watch was not unusual. I often felt I was being only barely tolerated and my questions answered as if they were rather ridiculous. Gilroy (1992: xi) has noted that the battered concept of anti-racism means it is now a concept that is 'almost impossible to utter in the still, serious places where . . . formal processes operate. Its use reflects badly on the credibility of those who invoke it'. This has become particularly so with the ascendancy of (anti)'political correctness' discourses.

In an interview with a deputy director whose main responsibility was staffing, I had to wait outside his office for thirty minutes after the arranged time of our meeting and when I did go into his office he told me he would now only be able to see me for a very short period. As I hurriedly worked my way through the interview schedule and began to ask him questions as to NATFHE's role in relation to equality initiatives in the university, he demanded to know why I was talking about the union:

> *SN*: Perhaps we could move on and look at NATFHE . . .
> *DD*: (interrupts) Why do you want to talk to me about NATFHE?
> *SN*: Well, as I explained in my letter and at the beginning, my research has a focus on the role . . .
> *DD*: (interrupts) Of?
> *SN*: On the role of NATFHE and the AUT in equal opportunities development in higher education – do you see NATFHE as having such a role?
> *DD*: Right. Nothing comes to mind. Neither positive nor negative.
> *SN*: What sort of profile does NATFHE have at the university then?
> *DD*: Why do you choose NATFHE – we have three separate unions?
> *SN*: Because my interest is in academic white collar unions . . .
> *DD*: (interrupts) The APTC is a white collar trade union.
> *SN*: Yes, but NATFHE is a much larger academic union and the research has to be selective.
> *DD*: Right. OK. But as I say, NATFHE is but one of three unions here.

While the aggressive tone in which this respondent challenged me in this interview is not conveyed in the extract itself, the hostility of the respondent can be seen in a number of connected ways: the continual interruptions, not letting me finish explanations and a refusal to accept the validity of the research focus even after I had offered explanations. It is also significant that this respondent who had emphasized his limited amount of time at the beginning of the interview was then able to take time to question me in this way.

In another incident, a new vice-chancellor had taken over one of the 'new' university case studies near the end of my fieldwork. I wrote to him explaining my research and requesting an interview. He later agreed to this. As soon as I was in his office, he demanded to know who had given me permission to use the university as a case study and who I had spoken to so far. Through this interviewing of me, I felt it was clearly implied by the vice-chancellor that he wouldn't have allowed me access. When I explained which groups I was interested in talking to in the university, but reminded him that all my respondents were unnamed and anonymous, the situation became very confrontational. Although I thought/hoped that the interview wouldn't go ahead, the vice-chancellor did allow me to ask him some questions. As with the above excerpt, the following excerpt from the transcript is significant because it also provides an illustration of the struggle for control of the interview process:

SN: What is your own understanding or definition of the concept of equal opportunities?
VC: You must know the literature on equal opportunities.
SN: Yes, but what is your personal view?
VC: Equal opportunities is what it says it is.
SN: What would you say it was?
VC: Equality of opportunity. You can't produce equality of outcome. You've got to distinguish between running an institution of higher education and improving the condition of mankind.

These excerpts are also significant in that they demonstrate simultaneously both the respondents' hostility towards me and their hostility to the nature of the questions I asked. Such experiences take an emotional toll and after many interviews I would seek the safe, autonomous space of the women's toilets to sit and recover.

Conclusion

At the beginning of this chapter, I quoted from Stanfield (1993: xii) as to the 'reluctance of researchers studying controversial areas to provide auto-biographical statements', and as Gramsci has noted, 'the starting point of critical evaluation is the consciousness of what one really is' (quoted in Said, 1978: 25). By writing in (my)self, this chapter has examined the tensions which can arise from trying simultaneously to employ both anti-racist and (traditional) feminist approaches in the field. There is a process of reconciliation that has to be negotiated between the reciprocal, subjective tenets of the feminist approach and the challenging, oppositional tenets of the anti-racist approach. While the two are not exclusive of each other, the masculinity of the anti-racist stance does not always sit easily with the femininity of the feminist stance. My own (unresolved) process of reconciliation was made more problematic because of the nature of my research site, which involved an upwards gaze. In other words, it was not always possible (or desirable) to be egalitarian, reciprocal and subjective when interviewing powerful and overwhelmingly male professionals. Conversely, it was not always possible (if desirable) to be dissenting and confrontational when interviewing the same powerful and overwhelmingly male professionals. While there has been some feminist commentary on the difficulties in sustaining a feminist research approach (Smart, 1984; Gewirtz and Ozga, 1993), this has not addressed a race dimension. Similarly, Back and Solomos (1992), Solomos and Back (1995) and Keith (1992) have noted the complexities of being (confrontational) anti-racist researchers but have not incorporated a gender dimension into these discussions. What I have attempted to address are the (emotional) processes of compromise and distortion of both my anti-racist and feminist identities in my research practice. The chapter does not seek to 'excuse' these compromises or distortions, nor give any 'right way' of conducting anti-racist, feminist research. Rather, the chapter attempts to highlight the myriad of complexities that lie behind the intention to, or the assertion of, doing anti-racist, feminist research and the impossibility of 'sustaining one ethical position in all contexts' (Back and Solomos, 1992: 25).

2

The Changing Face of Higher Education in Britain

Introduction

This chapter traces how the higher education system in Britain has moved, since 1945, via successive Conservative and Labour government policies, from an elitist model towards an expansionist model. It questions to what extent social justice concerns motivated post-war higher education policy and explores the nature of the tensions that the expansionist process has engendered in the academy. While it is clear that previously excluded groups have secured a place in the contemporary British higher education sector, the second part of the chapter draws on the existing higher education and equal opportunities research to argue that higher education's response to the presence of these groups and to equality policy generation and implementation remains ambiguous. The final section of the chapter introduces four university case studies in which the fieldwork was conducted.

Elite formulations of higher education

The pre-industrial or medieval construction of a higher education system centred on the idea of a select, and necessarily, few (men) entering architecturally beautiful buildings and completely immersing themselves in the processes of learning and attaining the highest levels of knowledge, truth and scholarship. The concerns of these few were understood to be abstract rather than material, and in many ways poverty and learning sat easily beside each other (see, for example, Chaucer's *Clerke's Tale*, 1908).

Although the industrial revolution forced this to change, certain aspects of the medieval university model were to remain intact, mainly the notion that higher education was only for the select (privileged) few. It was this construction that was not only able to evolve to meet the requirements of capitalist modernity, but to become essential to it. In the nineteenth and early twentieth centuries, higher education had a clear position in capitalist organized social relations and a close affinity with the ruling classes and their interests.

Despite the modern universities' relationship with capitalism, the interpretation of higher education as an intellectual assembly line for the production of members of the ruling classes is too crude. The relationship is made more complex by the second legacy of the medieval university model, the importance of knowledge. This duality between furnishing the needs of the economic and class system and the pursuit (and cultural benefits) of knowledge has dominated the debates and developments of higher education over the last one hundred years. The central project of higher education has been to converge this duality. For example, in his inaugural speech at St Andrews University, John Stuart Mill argued that:

> The university is not a place of professional education. Universities are not intended to teach the knowledge required to fit men for some special mode of gaining their livelihood ... Men are men before they are lawyers or physicians or merchants or manufacturers: and if you make them capable and sensible men, they make themselves capable and sensible lawyers or physicians.
>
> (Stuart Mill, 1963: 312–13)

The notion of the sanctity of university education and of learning as a cultural process was similarly echoed by Newman (1959). The emphasis was on the production of cultivated people and an elite rather than on the production of expert people.

Central to higher education's production of a cultivated elite was the issue of who was allowed access to it. Inevitably, access was characterized by restriction. Even as recently as the beginning of the 1980s, 'Britain had only seven students in its universities for every thousand of the population, the lowest proportion in Europe and about one-sixth that of the United States' (Halsey, 1992: 11). Through restricted access and emphasis on learning as a cultural resource, higher education and its institutions were able to maintain their remoteness and seeming autonomy from industrial Britain.

However, since 1945, higher education has increasingly faced social and economic demands to change. Social in terms of the post-war ascendancy of the notion of, and desire for, meritocracy (the creation of the Welfare State, the 1944 Education Act), and economic in terms of the need for a more widely trained (especially in the areas of science and technology) labour force. As Salter and Tapper (1994) argue, higher education's overwhelming financial reliance on the state meant that the sector had to go some way at least, mainly via expansion, towards meeting these social and economic demands.

Although I address expansionism below, I think it is important to argue that the elite model of the university, if in a modified version, has not only survived, but has much currency in the discourses which surround contemporary higher education (Hague, 1990; Allington and O'Shaughnessy, 1992).

Higher education in the post-war period: elitism to expansionism to massification

With the post-war ascendancy of the notion of meritocracy, access to universities served as a stark indicator of social inequality. Accompanying meritocratic demands has been a desire on the part of the state to bring higher education more under its control. Salter and Tapper (1994) have argued that the state has employed a variety of strategies by which to achieve this: 'legal, financial, administrative and most importantly of all, ideological' (p. 5). At the ideological level, this struggle can be seen to be played out between the need to have higher education relating more directly to the economic requirements of the state – the production of trained workers – and the elite role of higher education – the production of a 'civilized' and 'cultural' class who would disinterestedly pursue knowledge and take up elevated social positions. The irony of this ideological struggle can be seen in the state's requirement that higher education fulfil both these tasks and in the close relationship between the state and the academy who were 'joined by a seamless web of shared understanding and values' (Salter and Tapper, 1994: 8).

Initially, this situation was cautiously approached, first with the Robbins Report (1963) and then through the creation of a binary higher education system in 1966. It was not until the advent of the New Right and the 1979 election of a Conservative administration that the relationship between higher education and the state became more overtly antagonistic. For example, Halsey (1992: 254–5, table 11.4) found that 90 per cent of professors believed that the government should have less control of universities. It is the initial tentative expansionist strategies that I now explore.

The Robbins Report

Although expansion within higher education had been underway since the beginning of the twentieth century (Halsey, 1992; see, for example, the establishment of the redbrick universities), the establishment of the Robbins Committee in the early 1960s and the Robbins Report (1963) was *ideologically* significant because it represented expansion as *formal* government policy. Despite the report's all-important assertion of the principle that 'courses of higher education should be available for all those who are qualified by ability and attainment to pursue them and who wished to do so' (Robbins, 1963: 7–8), expansionism under Robbins remained faithful to the elite model of the university. Emphasizing the need for academic freedom and autonomy, the report identified four key objectives for higher education: 'the need for instruction in skills relevant for the general divisions of labour'; the education of 'not mere specialists but rather cultivated men and women'; 'the advancement of learning'; and 'the transmission of a common culture and common standards of citizenship' (Robbins, 1963: 6–7). Of these, only the 'instruction of skills' objective dissented from the traditional role of higher education. The report's tilt towards a continuing subscription to the elite model of the university and away from an economic/ vocational orientated higher education model was further emphasized in its warning that educational investment could not be 'measured adequately by the same yardstick as investment in coal or electricity' (Robbins, 1963: 205; Salter and Tapper, 1994).

While the Robbins Report was accepted and can be closely associated with the beginning of the expansionism of higher education, the direction of the report's sympathies and its projected scale of expansion was out of step with the economic and social requirements of the time. As Salter and Tapper (1994: 18) note: 'Modern economies require an ever-changing blend of new knowledge and educated manpower if they are to function effectively and no state can afford to leave its higher education system to its own devices'. Just over two years after the Robbins Report, a White Paper, *A Plan for Polytechnics and Other Colleges*, appeared which called for the establishment of a binary higher education system.

Polytechnics and public sector higher education

The 1965 White Paper announced the creation of thirty polytechnics out of the twenty-five old regional colleges and established the binary division of higher education in Britain. The emergence of polytechnics formally represented the ascendancy of the economically orientated system of higher education and its location within the public sector made higher education both accountable to economic needs and provided the terrain in which such a system could be managed efficiently. The polytechnics represented a form of government pressure on the 'other' universities to provide more closely for the economic and/or public interest. Polytechnics were intended to be more firmly planned than the universities. Giles (1977) argues that the polytechnics were 'children of the towns or town councils, administrative bodies which wanted to administer the new institutions, to press them and keep them in the mould which they saw as most appropriate to the demands of the cities' (quoted in Becher and Kogan, 1992: 31).

From their conception, then, polytechnics were expected to provide a different kind of higher education to that of the universities. Polytechnics operated on a policy of far more open access and a substantial proportion of their degree courses provided by polytechnics tended to be vocationally, technically and practically orientated, in contrast to the academic and disciplinary courses offered by universities. Social relevance, then, was to become the pivot on which public sector higher education was to be established.

It was a policy that had party political consensus, for example Margaret Thatcher's 1972 White Paper, *Education: A Framework for Expansion,* which endorsed Labour policy, emphasized the need for higher education to be economically relevant and 'looked to the polytechnics to play a key role in the expansion of the 1970s' (Halsey, 1992: 112; Becher and Kogan, 1992: 31).

However, the vision of separate and divided, but equal, higher education systems was to prove elusive. As early as 1974, Burgess and Pratt identified the 'academic drift' of the public sector towards the traditional university model, and Becher and Kogan (1992: 31) argue that 'the case of the polytechnics demonstrates that the basic characteristics of higher education cannot be easily overridden'. Similarly, Salter and Tapper (1994: 4) highlight the problematic fusion of higher education with economic need and argue that the 'academic drift' of polytechnics represented 'a salutary tribute to the power of universities and an example of why the state has to trade with them'.

The universities, although still entrenched in and guarding their commitment to 'academic freedom' and 'autonomy', have made moves towards meeting identifiable market needs (Hague, 1990; Russell, 1993). At certain levels, then, the boundaries of the division had become blurred by the 1980s. By 1987–88, there were equal numbers of full-time students in both sectors. Yet other divisions, connected with prestige, status and the recruitment of the mythical 'students of high quality', had become more marked, establishing a hierarchy, or 'ladder', of higher education. For example, Halsey (1992: 115) quotes a polytechnic head of department who claimed that 'virtually every student would rather be at a university'. Whether or not such a claim has any empirical validity is not really the issue. Rather, such statements act as indicators of the extent of the cultural division of the sector, the very depth of which must question the ability of legislation alone to produce a unified system. Although Hague (1990) lamented what he called the 'Spitfire snobbery' of the system, he was keen to preserve the polytechnic/university divide, and ironically stated that 'today many polytechnics yearn to become universities and, if the present system survives, one day some politician will be daft enough to let them' (p. 71). Allington and O'Shaughnessy (1992: 110) offer an unequivocal defence of a binary system: 'privilege has to be earned . . . "Technical Universities" should still imply that all-important differentiation of function, without making polytechnic students and staff feel alienated'. They attack the 'academic drift' of the polytechnics, stating with undisguised outrage that 'North London Polytechnic employs eight lecturers in philosophy, four less than the University of Cambridge' (p. 109). The cultural chasm between universities and polytechnics, which is both real and imagined, has been highlighted by Halsey (1992: 117–21).

Both the cultural and structural divides between the polytechnics and the university sector have provided the focus for post-1979 Conservative policy approaches towards the higher education system.

Conservative higher education policy since 1979

The relative failure of the binary system, reflected in the seduction of polytechnics by non-market university values and the 'loose canon' nature of the university sector (i.e. its relatively autonomous location within the state structure and its association with leftist thinking), represented a situation which not surprisingly elicited the immediate hostility of an incoming Conservative administration which was intent on pursuing a New Right political agenda.

The period from 1979 to 1994 was one in which the Conservative Government pursued an overtly hostile policy strategy for increasing state control of higher education within a continued and, according to New Right thinking, a more energetic and distinctive ideological framework of harnessing the system to the marketplace. In the early 1980s, this strategy took the form of dramatic cuts in the financing of higher education (Kogan and Kogan, 1983). In the late 1980s and early 1990s, this strategy culminated in the equally dramatic 1988 Education Reform Act and the 1992 Further and Higher Education Act. The 1988 Education Act instituted fundamental changes in the ways in which the state funded higher education. The Act removed polytechnics from local authority control, replacing the National Advisory Body for Public Sector Higher Education (NAB) by the Polytechnics and Colleges Funding Council (PCFC). In relation to the university sector, the 1988 Act replaced the University Grants Committee (UGC), a body first established in 1919 to act as a 'buffer' between the state and higher education (see Salter and Tapper, 1994: 104–33). In place of the UGC, the Act created the University Funding Council (UFC). Both these funding councils were placed more directly under the control of the Department of Education and Science and the Secretary of State for Education. While the polytechnic sector welcomed the move to free them from local authority control, the universities were more hostile to the new funding system, fearing for their autonomy. The ideological thrust behind the Act was one which pushed universities and polytechnics into a position of competing and earning their own rewards in the academic marketplace (Becher and Kogan, 1992) within a 'framework of ministerial directives designed to ensure that the public received value-for-money in return for the Exchequer's input' (Salter and Tapper, 1994: 204).

In many ways, the 1992 Further and Higher Education Act reinforced the provisions of the 1988 Education Reform Act. Most significantly, the 1992 Act ended the binary higher education system through the merging of the two funding councils into the Higher Education Funding Councils for England, Wales and Scotland. Polytechnics were allowed to apply for university status and this was widely and successfully taken up by those institutions. The ending of the formal division between polytechnics (offering vocationally or professionally orientated higher education) and universities (offering a traditional liberal or elite academically orientated higher education) can be understood within an ideological framework, that the higher education system relate more specifically to economic and market needs. Although the division may remain at a cultural level (see, for example, Halsey, 1992), this division is strictly contained within a rubric of financial and ministerial control. That research activities and teaching quality within universities have come under four yearly scrutiny (and possible sanction) has to be understood within the legislative framework of the 1988 and 1992 Acts.

It is vital that the provisions of the 1988 and 1992 Acts be understood within the political objective of creating a higher education system more completely under government control. The strategies towards higher education pursued by successive Conservative administrations over sixteen years represent the successful culmination of post-war attempts to bring higher education more securely under government control and relate the activities of higher education more closely to economic and market needs. What I explore below is the impact that the post-war developments in higher education have had in terms of equal opportunities.

Higher education expansion, social justice and access

The key question to be explored here is whether the fundamental changes in the higher education system in the post-war period – most obviously, its expansion – have meant the creation of access routes to those groups previously excluded from higher education (i.e. working-class people, women and black and other minority ethnic groups). It is, in many ways, an easy equation to relate expansionism and the post-binary system with greater equality, and Halsey (1992: 267) has argued that 'a programme of expansion assuaged the guilt of exclusion of the mass of working class compatriots'. Yet it is problematic to interpret the changing face of higher education as atonement for exclusion. I have argued above that the political ideology behind post-war government policy approaches has been forged through the need to bring higher education under greater state control and harness higher education to the demands of the marketplace. The political ideology has not been based on the desire for greater social justice within higher education. That there are now routes of access into higher education for previously excluded groups has to be viewed as a 'by-product' of these policies rather than their original or primary intention. As Tapper and Salter (1978: 176) argue, 'it has been one of the more accepted fallacies of current educational thought that higher education was at least partly expanded to achieve equality of education for the working classes'.

There is an uneasy relationship between the academy and the presence of working-class people, women and black and other minority ethnic groups within it, as indicated by the rise of the 'declining standards' discourse that has much currency within the academy. For example, Allington and

O'Shaughnessy (1992: 107) argue that 'it is an idle . . . pretence to maintain that such a large [student] cohort can be admitted without lowering standards'. The notion that 'academic excellence' has been eroded via the expansion of higher education is one which contains the sub-text that 'academic excellence' has been eroded by the inclusion of previously excluded groups. While I have argued above that Conservative higher education policies have been largely successful in their efforts to increase both control over the higher education system and its market orientation, I have also noted that the legacy of the elite university model remains a powerful influence on the entire higher education system, and this has become more rather than less acute in the post-binary era. It is reflected in cultural divisions between the 'old' and the 'new' universities and in the contemporary landscape of higher education in which prestige, status, 'high-quality' students and 'academic excellence' are increasingly sought after labels for higher education institutions. In the competing marketplace, these act as invaluable assets. Within this context, the tendency for 'new' universities is to equalize upwards and emulate the 'old' universities as they move to shed those 'traditional' features associated with public sector higher education provision. Chapter 6 discusses how this theme emerged a number of times in the 'new' university case studies when senior management respondents would often refer to their concerns that the 'new' sector was seen by the 'old' sector as comprising 'mickey mouse' universities.

The point I am making is that while expansion may have opened up access routes to previously excluded groups (although this is not to deny that access remains a specific issue; Leicester, 1993), social justice concerns were not the motivation behind expansionist policies. Consequently, the presence – or rather the associations of the presence – of these groups in higher education has elicited an ambiguous response from the academy. Before looking in more detail at the existing research as to this response, I first consider the gender and race dimensions of the changing face of higher education in contemporary Britain.

Gender dimensions

There has always been a historical proximity between women and education, specifically in terms of teaching. From the isolated, miserable lives of nineteenth-century governesses to their contemporary over-representation as primary school teachers, for white, predominantly middle- and upper-class (i.e. respectable) women, teaching has been constructed as a suitable and therefore feminine career. However, women's entry into higher education was both slow and resisted. In 1869, London University became the first higher education institution to admit women students, a fact that is highlighted in the university's current equal opportunities statement. What is omitted from the statement is that women students in this period were only allowed to take modified versions of the degree examinations being taken by male students. It was not until the 1890s, when women's colleges had been established at Oxbridge, that the granting of degrees in most of the major universities was equalized (Halsey, 1992: 219).

In the first half of the twentieth century, women who did manage to enter higher education institutions and take up a professional career did so by placing themselves outside of a marriage and family relationship (Delamont, 1978). The difficulties reconciling an academic career with domestic responsibilities remain today (see Blackstone and Fulton, 1974, 1975; Simeone, 1987; Leonard and Malina, 1994). In 1989, a far greater proportion of male academics were married in comparison to women academics and a far higher number of women academics were either divorced or separated (Halsey, 1992: 224, table 10.2). Such findings indicate the persistence of the conflict for (heterosexual) women between the domestic and the professional spheres. The academy has tended to resist the creation of a space in which the public and private spheres of female academics' lives are able to converge. For example, Leonard and Melina (1994: 30) argue that:

> Being a mother in academic life is a predominantly silent experience. The facts of this motherhood – the personal struggles, compromises and solutions to the daily problem of attempting to combine being a good mother and a competent, productive academic – are largely unvoiced at work.

Significantly, however, the public/private divide has been recognized within the academy to the extent that it is reproduced in a gendered academic division of labour. Women academics spend a greater proportion of their time in the more pastoral-orientated teaching of undergraduates than in conducting research and knowledge production, and male academics are more likely to supervise research students than their female colleagues (Halsey, 1992: 224, table 10.2).

The expansion of higher education in the post-war period did impact directly on the numbers of women entering the sector as students. According to Halsey (1992: 101, table 4.6), between 1970 and 1988–89, the number of full-time male undergraduates increased by 11,400, whereas the number of full-time female undergraduates increased by 52,700. Halsey's figures are also interesting because they show that in the early years of the polytechnics, full-time female students outnumbered full-time male students by almost 11,000. That majority has slowly been reduced and by 1988–89 male students comprised the larger group: 147,900 men compared with 146,700 women (Halsey, 1992: 101, table 4.6). In offering the opportunity to study for a degree on a part-time basis, public sector institutions (and the Open University) provided candidates with new routes into higher education. Such a provision had specific relevance for women and especially women with dependants. Again Halsey's figures bear witness to this. Between 1970 and 1988–89, the total number (university, polytechnic and Open University) of male part-time students increased by 88,600, while for female part-time students the increase was 132,000, indicating the substantial gender differences in the uptake of part-time degree study (Halsey, 1992: 101, table 4.6).

While it is clear that there has been a mass entry of women into higher education in the post-war period, it is crucial to look beyond simply the visibility of women and focus on the areas where they are visible. There is still an overwhelming propensity for women students to enter academic disciplines where they have traditionally been tolerated, for example the arts and humanities, or those which conform to gender occupation stereotypes, for example teaching and nursing. Although the proportion of women re-entering higher education as academics has increased, their locations within the disciplinary spectrum tend to reflect these gender divisions. The vast majority of women academics are in the social science and arts disciplines, with still only a fraction of women in the 'natural' sciences and engineering and technology (Halsey, 1992: 224, table 10.2). Academic hierarchies within higher education institutions are also starkly gendered. At the base of the structure, women make up the majority of lecturers after which their presence goes into a steep decline: only 8.9 per cent of readers and senior lecturers are women compared with 22.3 per cent of men, and a mere 1.7 per cent of professors are women in contrast to 11.4 per cent of men (Halsey, 1992: 222, table 10.1). Similarly, figures from the AUT *Update* survey (1993) showed that less than one in twenty of Britain's 'top' academics are women, a significant discrepancy considering the number of women students and academics. In 1991, the AUT conducted an audit of the salaries of academic staff. This highlighted how women earned comparatively less than male academics. For example, the audit revealed that on average, female academics earn only 83.9 per cent of male academics' salaries. The central reason for these pay differences is the concentration of women in the lower grades (AUT, 1992; Bagilhole, 1994).

Clearly women have entered higher education, both as students and as academics, in the post-war period, but gender discrepancies in terms of where and at what levels expose a system of effective gatekeeping. For example, the *Hansard Report* (1990: 68) described universities as 'bastions of male power and privilege' and even suggested that the under-representation of women in top positions should elicit the attention of the Equal Opportunities Commission.

It is also important to ask what kind of women have made the journey into higher education. Empirical data are scarce in this respect. Halsey's statistics in relation to academics reveal that the vast majority are middle-class women from middle-class backgrounds. That there is a slightly larger percentage of male academics than female academics who have a manual-class background would seem to indicate that there is a higher degree of struggle for working-class women to enter the academy. It is significant that neither in Halsey's otherwise comprehensive survey of academics or in the AUT's research, there are no references, quantitative or qualitative, to ethnicity or race. It is to this issue that I now turn.

Race dimensions

In contrast to the array of statistics concerning the number and location of women academics, there is far less statistical knowledge concerning the number and location of black and other minority ethnic academics. Figures released by the Higher Education Statistics Agency for 1994–95 revealed that 6.62 per cent of the known academic staff population in higher education identified themselves as belonging to a minority ethnic category. However, this figure should be treated with caution, as the known academic staff population is only 61.67 per cent of the total population. Consequently, the 6.62 per cent of minority ethnic academics is likely to be actually much lower (Abbassi, 1996). There has been a wider statistical examination of black and minority students entering higher education (Modood, 1993a, 1993b; Small, 1994; Skellington, 1996). In the early 1990s, the Polytechnics Central Admissions System (PCAS) and the Universities Central Clearing and Admissions (UCCA) system began to collect data which monitored ethnicity and student applications. This data revealed that African/Caribbean and Bangladeshi applications were significantly under-represented in the old university sector (see Taylor, 1992; UCCA *Statistical Supplementary Report*, 1991–92). The PCAS ethnicity monitoring data revealed that 86.6 per cent of all applicants were white men and women, compared to 13.4 per cent of African/Caribbean and South Asian descent. The data also showed that 85.6 per cent of all admissions went to white men and women, compared to 14.4 per cent of those of African/Caribbean and Asian descent (cited in Henry, 1994: 47). Modood (1993a) has argued that the overall PCAS and UCCA figures do not substantiate claims of under-representation of black and other minority ethnic applications, but notes that they confirm differential rates of selection between 'new' and 'old' universities (see also CRE, 1988). As Small (1994: 68) argues 'black students are not well represented, and certainly not over-represented, in universities'. A more recent survey conducted on minority ethnic graduates (*Labour Market Trends*, 1996) reported that of all British students in the (publicly funded) British higher education system, 12 per cent identified themselves as belonging to a minority ethnic group. While this figure is significant, as it is almost double the minority ethnic population percentage as a whole, the survey revealed discrepancies in the spread of minority ethnic graduates across the higher education sector. For example, there was a higher concentration of minority ethnic graduates who had completed their degrees at 'new' universities, there were regional variations and differential rates of success for minority ethnic students (Heward and Taylor, 1993; Abbassi, 1996; Law, 1996).

While there is an obvious need for continuing and more statistical data concerning both black and minority ethnic students and academics, the insight offered by such quantitative data is limited. The documentation of the experiences of black and other minority ethnic students and academics within the higher education system equally requires urgent attention. While the Oxford Students Union Survey, 1994 (cited in *The Times*, 8 December,

1994) provides some indication of experiences of racism in higher education in Britain, it has been left to such black feminist writers as hooks (1989), Williams (1992), Henry (1994), Mirza (1995), and Nkweto Simmonds (1997) to provide more qualitative (and personalized) accounts of the complexity of black experience of higher education in the United States and Britain. For example, Patricia Williams (1992: 167) recounts how:

> At a Faculty meeting once, I raised several issues: racism among my students, my difficulty in dealing with it myself and my need for support from colleagues. I was told by a white professor that 'we' should be able to 'break the anxiety by just laughing about it.' Another nodded in agreement and added that 'the key is not to take this sort of thing too seriously'.

This reveals much more about the experiences of being a black woman in higher education than any statistical figures as to the proportion of black women currently in higher education can.

While it is clearly possible to argue that the expansion of higher education in the post-war period has created routes of access for previously excluded groups, the entryism of such groups can only be the starting point for any consideration of their experiences within the academy. What I now want to examine, by drawing on the existing research and literature in the area, is the anti-discriminatory (policy) responses that higher education has made to the presence of women and black and other minority ethnic students and academics and to broader issues of equality within the sector.

Higher education and equal opportunities policies

Equal opportunities issues have secured a place on higher education's agendas. This place is demonstrated by such developments as the CVCP's *Guidelines on Equal Opportunities in Employment* (1991) and the CVCP's establishment of the Commission on University Career Opportunity (CUCO) in 1993 (see also CUCO, 1994; *Equal Opportunities Review*, 1995; Farish *et al.*, 1995). However, it is the *centrality* (or otherwise) of that place on higher education's agenda that needs to be examined. What also requires examination is the substance and types of equality policies that have been generated in the higher education sector. In the following section, the chapter focuses on these questions by drawing on the existing literature. Chapters 5 and 6 take this examination further by analysing equal opportunities policy-making and implementation in the four university case studies.

Despite the legislative ending of the binary system of higher education, the binary divide between the old universities and the former polytechnics or new universities remains an important aspect in any consideration of equality initiatives and policies in higher education and this is reflected in the literature that exists in the area (Williams *et al.*, 1989; Jewson *et al.*,

1991, 1993; Farish *et al.*, 1995). The former polytechnic sector has been more extensively associated with a commitment to equal opportunities and to providing routes into higher education for 'non-traditional' students. For example, Craft and Craft (1983) (reflecting the statistical evidence: *Labour Market Trends*, 1996) have argued that black school leavers were more likely than their white counterparts to attend polytechnics rather than universities when choosing a higher education course. The research of Jewson *et al.* (1993), which studied 32 polytechnic prospectuses for references to equal opportunities commitments, found that just under half (47 per cent) of institutions made explicit reference to equality policies. Jewson and his colleagues have argued on the basis of this research that 'it is difficult not to conclude that the polytechnics offered a more extensive and overt commitment to formal equal opportunities policies than universities' (p. 8). The association of the former polytechnic sector with equality issues can be understood in the combined context of a history of local authority control, the types of courses offered, more flexible entry requirements and the geographical locations of polytechnics, which were often in urban, industrialized areas. In other words, it is important to locate the closer relationship between the former polytechnic sector and equal opportunities to circumstantial reasons, rather than a primary political motivation on the part of polytechnic institutions to address social justice concerns. For example, Williams *et al.* (1989: 15, table 2) found that the most commonly cited reason for polytechnic institutions' take up of an equal opportunities agenda was local authority pressure. In the post-binary, market-orientated system of higher education, this relationship begins to look increasingly vulnerable (see above). As Jewson *et al.* (1993: 5) note:

> Now that old polytechnics have disappeared and the newly created universities are seeking to find their identities, it is of vital importance to preserve and enhance the best practises with respect to equal opportunities. Moreover, reorganisation and redesignation represents an opportunity to review and enhance policies in the higher education sector as a whole.

Given that the 'old' university sector has operated within a different ideological context of higher education provision, it is not surprising that its incorporation of an equal opportunities agenda has been a slower and more reticent process.

The research by Williams *et al.* (1989: 12) found that of the forty-two 'old' universities questioned, twenty cited their institutional charter as sufficient evidence of their commitment to equal opportunities issues and anti-discriminatory practice. Such charters are characteristically vague and tend to claim that discrimination only occurs on the basis of 'merit' and 'ability' and make scant, if any, reference to equal opportunities specifically. Although thirteen universities stated the existence of equality policies or a declaration of (anti-discriminatory) intent, none provided evidence of either the policy documents or of their implementation (Williams *et al.*, 1989: 11, table 1).

Significantly, this research found evidence of the notion that by implementing equal opportunities, institutions would be seen to be relaxing 'standards' to facilitate access for 'non-traditional' students (p. 12).

The inadequate response of the 'old' university sector to equal opportunities concerns, which Williams and co-workers' survey highlights, was similarly echoed in the work of Jewson *et al.* (1991). Surveying fifty-three university prospectuses for references to equal opportunities policies or provisions, Jewson *et al.* were only able to identify four which included statements which explicitly referred to an equal opportunities policy at the institution. Seven university prospectuses contained statements referring to admissions/recruitment criteria being academically based. The remaining forty-two prospectuses in the sample 'contained no statement which the researchers felt able to classify as either embodying or implying an equal opportunities commitment' (Jewson *et al.*, 1991: 187).

This research is both interesting and significant: a prospectus is essentially an advertising package for an institution. In having the photographic depictions of black and other minority ethnic groups within the prospectuses (which were generally widespread) as a focal concern of the research project, Jewson *et al.* were able to highlight the contrast between the more immediate visual portrayals of harmonious, 'multi-racial' institutions with the perhaps less obvious absence of textual references to commitment to the equal opportunities concept and/or initiatives for the promotion and implementation of equal opportunities practice.

Both Williams *et al.* (1989) and Jewson *et al.* (1991, 1993) illuminate a degree of resistance to the formulation and implementation of equal opportunities policy and practice, especially within the 'old' university sector. However, there is a danger in representing an over-simplified picture of equal opportunities in higher education – that is, that the former polytechnics have been willing to incorporate an equal opportunities agenda, whereas the 'old' universities have been more reluctant to address equality issues. I noted earlier that the polytechnics' apparent willingness to take up equal opportunities has to be contextualized (historically) and it cannot be assumed that all polytechnic institutions have positively responded to equality issues, but rather that there have been 'pockets of good practice' (MacGregor, 1990). The CVCP guidelines on *Equal Opportunities in Employment in Universities* (1991) and the establishment of COCU in 1993 signify new moves within the 'old' universities towards an admittance of the need to address equal opportunities and anti-discriminatory practices (Leicester, 1993; *Equal Opportunities Review*, 1995; Farish *et al.*, 1995). The more recent findings of the 1993 CUCO survey of 106 'old' universities reveal a shift in the approach of these institutions towards equal opportunities issues. The high response rate (97 per cent) and the high number of institutions which had formal equal opportunities statements (93 per cent) indicate a wider engagement of 'old' universities with equality concerns. Of the institutions surveyed, 79 per cent had harassment policies, 72 per cent had issued guidelines on recruitment and selection procedures and 82 per cent had a senior member with responsibility for implementing equality policies. However, it is important to note that only 42 per cent provided training in equal opportunities for staff responsible for recruitment and only 21 per cent of institutions made such training compulsory (CUCO, 1994). While such discrepancies are highly significant within the quantitative framework of the CUCO research, these cannot be qualitatively analysed. Similarly, the quantitative research of Williams *et al.* (1989) and Jewson *et al.* (1991, 1993) can only provide a limited insight into equal opportunities in higher education. The qualitative work of Farish *et al.* (1995) valuably highlights how complexity and contradiction impact on the effectiveness and ineffectiveness of equal opportunities policy-making, policy implementation and policy receivership in higher education institutions. Focusing on equal opportunities policies in relation to staff, Farish and her colleagues (1995: 180) suggest that the three organizations that they studied (a 'new' university, an 'old' university and a further education college) were 'interested primarily in projecting positive and progressive images of themselves, rather than in bringing about substantive changes which would genuinely enhance the employment opportunities of staff'. Farish *et al.* discovered that although their case-study institutions had engaged (often extensively) with equal opportunities concerns, 'those closely involved in the development of policies and practices ... found it difficult to point to concrete gains made as a result of their work' (p. 181). Reflecting the findings of other research into equal opportunities policies in organizations (see, for example, Cockburn, 1992), the work of Farish *et al.* (1995) and Heward and Taylor (1993) shows how the adoption of formal policies in relation to equal opportunities do not in themselves fundamentally affect the everyday workings of institutions. For example, Farish *et al.* found that despite the existence of equality policies, conventional patterns of staff employment – the dominance of white males in all senior positions – continued to exist in their case-study institutions.

While my own research builds on the findings of this significant, but still embryonic, literature, it also focuses on three areas that have as yet received little attention. First, there is a need to examine the limited nature of the equal opportunities discourse itself and its de-politicized character of equal opportunities in the 1990s (see, for example, Chapters 4 and 5). In particular, the place of race within equal opportunities policy generation in higher education requires consideration. Second, although Farish and her colleagues are concerned with the ways in which equal opportunities policies tend to fragment around certain areas and they note that race was an area which was particularly problematic for higher education institutions to develop good practice on, they do not focus on *why* race has such a problematic status (Chapters 1, 4 and 5). Similarly, while Leicester (1993) does focus on the issues of race and anti-racism in higher education, she approaches these issues in terms of emphasizing (and advocating) the importance of including race dimensions in the higher education teaching–learning model. Third, while there is an extensive body of literature which examines the (ambiguous) relationship of trade unions to equality issues (Wrench, 1986; Phizacklea and Miles, 1992; Chapter 3), there has been a lack of consideration in the higher education literature as to the role that academic trade unions (the AUT and NATFHE) have played in higher education's responses to equal opportunities issues. My research explores the AUT and NATFHE involvement with, and attitudes towards, equal opportunities policies in the four case-study universities.

The remainder of this chapter introduces these four universities by outlining the environment, course emphasis, staff and student profiles and the equal opportunities structures of each university.

Profile of four case studies

Northfield University: a 'new' university

This is a rapidly expanded university situated within walking distance of the centre of a medium-sized, relatively affluent town in northern England. Although the centre of the university is traditional red brick architecture, the expansion in student and staff numbers has entailed an extensive building programme and a split campus with sites scattered across the town. Given the size of the town and the location of the university, its physical presence and its students are very apparent. Although the town appears as predominantly white, the minority ethnic population is estimated to be between 9 and 10 per cent.[1]

The university caters for 15,000 students and consists of five main faculties: business, health, social sciences and law, design, and technology and science. University monitoring of the student body reveals that 50 per cent of students are female, 7 per cent are from minority ethnic backgrounds and 1.6 per cent have recognized special needs (1993 figures). The staff profile of the university reveals 47 per cent of staff are female and 3 per cent are from minority ethnic backgrounds.

The university has a very public equal opportunities face, a known commitment to the area and is associated with innovative equal opportunities practice. This is most obviously reflected in the university's extensive equal opportunities structures. These consist of a central Equal Opportunities Committee, which is chaired by the university's director. Three sub-committees for race equality, women and special needs, serve and advise the central Equal Opportunities Committee. The university has established two specialist units, the first of which is the Centre for Racial Equality (initially funded by Section 11 moneys[2]), which was created in 1987 and has one full-time worker and is overwhelmingly responsible for student issues and developing community links. The second is a Women's Unit, which was set up in 1992 and has two shared posts and is overwhelmingly responsible for staff issues. The university has created five equal opportunities posts within each faculty. The remit of these posts centres on students and curriculum development. The university has a full-time sexual harassment officer.[3] The officer reports directly to senior management and has institution-wide responsibility. The university has a Black Staff Group.

Castlebrook University: a 'new' university

Again, this is a very rapidly expanded university. It is located within one of the poorer inner London boroughs, which has an estimated minority ethnic population of around 24 per cent. Apart from the original large stone building, which is still the main centre of the university, the remaining university buildings are all new and although they are split site, the area across which they are located is a relatively small one.

The university caters for 17,000 students and has five main faculties: social sciences and law, education, science, business, and engineering and design. University monitoring figures state that 48 per cent of the student body is female and 19 per cent is from minority ethnic backgrounds. The university estimates that 1.67 per cent of its students have recognized special needs. In terms of staff profiles, 47 per cent are female and 2.7 per cent are from minority ethnic backgrounds (1992 figures).

Like Northfield University, Castlebrook University also has a public equal opportunities reputation. However, the association of the university with an equal opportunities commitment seems to have developed out of the university's ILEA legacy, its strong links with the local community and the existence of politicized factions within the staff and student body of the university, rather than institutionally based equality policies or initiatives. This is reflected in the university's very limited equal opportunities structure. This consisted of one small, senior management dominated central Equal Opportunities Committee, chaired by one of two pro-vice-chancellors, and a Disabilities Committee, which was primarily concerned with student issues.

Peoples University: an 'old' university

Peoples University is a relatively recent member of the 'old' university sector. While the university is multi-site, its main centre is located on the outskirts of a town in south east England, whose minority ethnic population is estimated to be around 5 per cent. Again this institution has undergone a process of rapid expansion in recent years and this is reflected architecturally. The original main building of the university is relatively small and stone-built. The remaining buildings are all modern.

With a student population in excess of 17,000, the university consists of ten faculties: arts, social science, education, maths, science, technology, management and business, health, modern languages and information, engineering and technology. Over half (56 per cent) of the students are female, while minority ethnic students account for under 4 per cent of the student body. Only 4.3 per cent of the university's students had recognized special needs. In terms of academic staff profiles, women accounted for 29 per cent and 1 per cent of university staff had recognized special needs. At the time of the research, no exact figures were available for monitoring academic staff by ethnicity, but the percentage was estimated to be very low (*Annual Equal Opportunities Report,* 1992).

Peoples University places a particular emphasis on providing access routes into higher education and this, coupled with innovative work around equality issues, has led to the institution having a high equal opportunities profile. Again one of the most immediate indicators of this is the extensive equal opportunities structure that the university has established since the late 1980s. This structure consists of an Equal Opportunities Committee, dominated by senior management and chaired in rotation by either the chancellor or one of two pro-vice-chancellors. The committee is served and advised by an Equal Opportunities Unit, which has responsibility for both student and staff issues. The Equal Opportunities Unit is headed by a senior level equal opportunities advisor and has a job-share full-time administrative post. Each university faculty has an equal opportunities convenor and a faculty-based Equal Opportunities Working Party. The university has a Black Staff Group and a Gay and Lesbian Staff Group.

Russell College: an 'old' university

Russell College is part of a traditional 'old' civic university located in an affluent, central area of a town in south east England. Architecturally, the college is mixed: its main building is modern but it also consists of nearby traditional buildings.

In comparison to the other case-studies, Russell College is small with a student population of just over 2500. The college is a specialized postgraduate institution and is departmentally rather than faculty organized. These departments incorporate both humanities and science disciplines.

At the time of the research, Russell College was just beginning to implement monitoring programmes for both its student and staff bodies. No exact figures were available in regard to gender, ethnicity or disability, although the college estimated that over half its student population was female with low percentages of minority ethnic students and students with special needs. Similarly, just under half of the academic staff were estimated to be female, with very low percentages of minority ethnic and disabled staff.

Russell College has no particular association with equal opportunities commitment or innovation. Conversely, however, the college did have a relatively extensive equal opportunities structure. This consisted of a large, central Equal Opportunities Working Group chaired by the college's director. Each department had a designated equal opportunities consultant and an Equal Opportunities Consultants Committee. The college had also created a part-time equal opportunities officer post whose remit was mainly student issues. The college has a Disabilities Committee. Equal opportunities concerns in relation to staff had been placed under the remit of the personnel department.

Conclusion

Higher education in Britain has travelled a significant distance from its early elite formations to its present mass formations. It is in the post-war period in which the greatest changes have occurred, as successive government policy strategies have sought to exercise a greater degree of control over universities and incorporate their function within a market and economic context. Initially, these strategies were relatively cautious and left university autonomy and elite (non-market) university values undisturbed. The advent of a Conservative administration in 1979 committed to New Right ideology, marked the beginning of a far more hostile policy approach to higher education. The swingeing financial cuts in the early 1980s, the 1988 Education Reform Act and the 1992 Further and Higher Education Act combined a package of policy measures which both curbed university autonomy and forced higher education into adopting a closer relationship with economic needs and the values of the marketplace. It has been the post-1979 Conservative approach to higher education in particular which has relocated higher education more centrally in contemporary society. While the expansion of the higher education system over the last fifty years has allowed previously excluded groups access to universities, I have emphasized that issues of equality and social justice were not instrumental in the generation of expansionist policy aims. However, the changing face of higher education has pushed the sector into a position in which it has been forced to engage with issues of equal opportunities. Although there are clear, quantitative indicators that higher education institutions have taken up policies in relation to equal opportunities, the limited qualitative research into the effectiveness of these policies reveals a more complex, ambiguous and contradictory picture, in which the adoption of formal policies appears to have had little fundamental impact on the everyday practices of institutions (Heward and Taylor, 1993; Farish *et al.*, 1995). My own research seeks to explore this complex picture further (Chapters 4 and 5). However, this chapter has also noted gaps in the existing higher education and equal opportunities literature, including a lack of attention paid to the position(s) that the AUT and NATFHE have taken up in relation to equality concerns in higher education. Like higher education, the trade union movement has also responded to equal opportunities in ambiguous ways. It is this response that the following chapter explores.

3

Uneasy Relationships: Trade Unionism, Equal Opportunities and Academic Political Consciousness

Introduction

The relationship between the trade union movement and issues of equal opportunities, particularly race, has long been characterized by ambiguity. For example, in the late nineteenth century, Ben Tillet, radical leader of the London dockers and a committed socialist, responded to the arrival of Jewish immigration at that time by stating, 'yes you are our brothers and we will stand by you, but we wish you had not come' (quoted in Meth, 1972: 5). During the twentieth century, the contradictions of the relationship between the trade union movement and race issues became more stark. Trade unions have campaigned for immigration controls, insisted on employment quotas for black workers, colluded with employers against black workers and refused to support black workers' industrial struggles (Fryer, 1984). As Wrench (1986: 3) notes, 'history shows the record of the trade union movement to be characterised at worst by appalling racism and often by an indefensible neglect of the issues of race and equal opportunity'. This chapter considers the contradictions of this relationship and, given the repositioning that the trade union movement has undergone regarding equality concerns since the late 1970s, questions to what extent trade unions can now be seen as sites in which equal opportunities issues receive support.

In both left and right political imaginations, trade unions have traditional leftist associations. However, these associations have been challenged. For example, there has been feminist commentary on the masculinist orientations of trade unionism (Beale, 1983; Cockburn, 1987, 1992). As Coote and Campbell (1987: 176) note:

the traditional priorities of union bargaining – focusing on the wage and the maintenance of differentials – have not helped lift women out of low paid areas or to alleviate their domestic responsibilities. On the contrary, they have primarily defended the interests of male workers.

Marxist theorists have also critically emphasized the defensive and reformist nature of trade unions and their accommodation into the capitalist economy (Luxemburg, 1900/1970; Lenin, 1902/1988; Gramsci, 1921/1978; Trotsky, 1929/1975; Hyman, 1971) For example, as J. Kelly (1988) has argued, for Gramsci, trade unions, particularly trade union bureaucracies, had to be viewed as a product of capitalism rather than an oppositional response to capitalism.

In the context of these critiques, the first part of this chapter foregrounds the shifting attitudes of the trade union movement towards the issues of race and equal opportunities. The chapter then explores white collar trade unionism and examines the history, profile and equal opportunities structures of the AUT and NATFHE and asks to what extent academics can be seen as specifically sympathetic and receptive to the equal opportunities agenda.

Trade unions and race

From 1945 until the early 1970s, the Trade Union Council (TUC) declared its approach towards black and minority ethnic workers as 'colour-blind' and argued that any special provisions for black workers would mean discrimination against white workers: 'the trade union movement is concerned with a man or woman as a worker. The colour of a man's skin has no relevance whatever to his work' (Vic Feather, General Secretary to the TUC, *Race Today*, August 1973). The official colour-blind response was combined with an emphasis on the need for integration and immigration controls. In other words, the response of the trade union movement reflected that of both Labour and Conservative administrations in this period (Solomos, 1993). While colour-blindness and integration may have constituted the official TUC line on black workers, individual trade unions at the local level were overtly engaged in exclusionary practices against black workers, entering into quota systems with employers and insisting on 'last hired, first fired' employment policies (Fryer, 1984; Ramdin, 1987; Wrench, 1986).

By the mid-1970s, a perceptible shift had occurred in the policy and pronouncements of the TUC in relation to black workers. This shift was marked by the replacement of a policy which had immigration control as its focus to a policy whose focus was racial discrimination. This was reflected most obviously in the establishment of the Equal Rights Committee and the Race Relations Advisory Committee within the TUC bureaucratic structures. A number of factors have been cited as being responsible for this repositioning of the TUC's approach to black workers: first, the increasing organization of opposition by white and black union activists and delegates to the 'colour-blind' integration policy (Miles and Phizacklea, 1977); second, the rise of the National Front in the mid-1970s – the far right was a traditional enemy of the working classes and therefore one the trade union movement felt comfortable in opposing (Knowles, 1992); third, a series of industrial disputes, predominantly involving black workers, that took place during the late 1960s and early 1970s (Miles and Phizacklea, 1977; Wrench, 1986, 1992). As Miles and Phizacklea (1978: 201) have argued:

> The strikes at Mansfield Hosiery and Imperial Typewriters did not sud-denly bring about an immediate reassessment of policy by the General Council but they did force certain trade union leaders to consider the issues, the necessary initial stage for any re-assessment of policy.

Other disputes included Courtaulds Red Scar Rayon Mill in 1965, Woolf Rubber Company in 1965 and Coneygre Foundry in 1967. These strikes were highly significant not only because they were instrumental in securing a change in policy on the part of the TUC, but also because they exposed the hostile and exclusionary attitudes of the trade union movement towards black workers; white workers crossed picket lines, the unions involved in these disputes often aligned themselves with management against the strikers and they refused to make strikes official.

While the move away from integration policies can be attributed to these industrial struggles, the rise of the National Front and dissent from activists within the movement, it is also important to understand this change as occurring in parallel with a changing approach on the part of the state in the same period.

The early years of the 1970s witnessed a debate as to the effectiveness of the 1965 and 1968 Race Relations Acts, which culminated in the 1976 Race Relations Act (Lester and Bindman, 1972; Smith, 1977). Participating in this debate in 1974 the TUC requested that its newly created Equal Rights Committee address a number of equal opportunity related tasks. These were predominantly education-orientated; for example, preparing union recruitment literature in minority ethnic languages, encouraging language training in English, encouraging equal opportunity dimensions in trade union education courses and examining the barriers to equal opportunity (Miles and Phizacklea, 1978). In 1976, the TUC and the Labour govern-ment ran a joint national campaign based on these issues and the Race Relations Act of that same year and the General Council of the TUC, in contrast to earlier positions, went on record stating:

> much needs to be done to eliminate the discrimination and disad-vantage facing ethnic minorities and for their part the General Council are advising affiliated unions about steps they should take to strengthen trade union organisation between immigrant and black workers and promote unity among working people.
>
> (*The Guardian*, 8 September 1976)

The new priorities given by the labour movement (trade unions and the Labour Party) to education and class unity can mainly be read as their response to the National Front and the presumed appeal of the far right to the (white) working class (Phizacklea and Miles, 1980). The labour movement interpreted racism as a condition that arose from negative social conditions and competition over scarce resources: 'the idea that adverse social conditions produced racism was labour's official policy . . . and was widely supported throughout the labour movement' (Knowles, 1992: 129). By associating racism with unemployment, poor housing and cuts in public expenditure, trade unions were able to place campaigns against racism within the more familiar terrain of labourist struggles. This strategy was to continue into the 1980s, although it was to become overlain by equal opportunity and anti-racist discourses.

The 1979 Conservative election victory had fundamental implications for the trade union movement for a number of reasons. First, the rise of the new right in mainstream politics diminished both the activities and appeal of the National Front (Nugent and King, 1979a; Solomos, 1993). The decline of the National Front in the national political landscape meant that the traditional focus of the trade union movement's anti-racist activity – the comfortable enemy of the far right – had been displaced. Second, the Thatcher administration was intent on disrupting the political consensus model within which the trade union movement had long been accommodated. The trade union movement now faced an overtly anti-trade union government. Third, in the aftermath of 1979, with the collapse of the parliamentary Labour Party, there was a realignment of the left which took place predominantly at a grass roots and local/municipal level and which pursued a political agenda that centred on seemingly 'non-class' issues of racism, sexism, gay and lesbian rights, and environmentalism.

Dominated by these shifts, the political complexion of the early and mid-1980s forced the trade union movement into a position of not only declaring a greater degree of commitment to a comprehensive programme of equal opportunities, but also into examining racism not simply as a component part of fascism but within the union movement itself. In 1981, Ken Gill, Chair of the TUC's Equal Rights Committee, argued that Congress policy now:

> Demands the removal of direct and indirect discrimination at the workplace; more, it demands that trade unions themselves look at their own structures and organisations and break down the barriers within the unions to advance black members to decision-making bodies, to executives and to officialdom. If in your industry or organisation there are no blacks, why? If there are no black lay or full-time officials, why? If there are no black activists, why? All these questions have to be asked within our movement.
>
> (quoted in Lancashire Association of Trades Councils, 1985: 6)

In the same year as this significant statement was made, the TUC launched the *TUC Charter for Equality of Opportunity for Black Workers* (to become known as the Black Workers' Charter and to be relaunched seven years later in

1988). This document contained a checklist for trade union organizations, recommending public declarations by individual unions of their commitment to equal opportunities; recommending that unions set up advisory committees and that they should give active encouragement to black members to become shop stewards, branch officials, regional and national officials. The Charter also urged trade unions to take equal opportunity orientated action around the issues of their recruitment, education schemes, publications, social activities and grievance procedures and recommended that unions:

> Review their rules and policies in order to ensure that union members are not allowed to use the trade union movement as a means of disseminating racist propaganda and ideas. Unions should also ensure that the myths and propaganda spread by racists are countered and the positive contribution that black workers make to industry and the union be emphasised.
>
> (TUC, 1981: 5)

The Charter proceeded to highlight the need for unions, as negotiators in collective bargaining, to include equal opportunity clauses in these procedures and agreements and emphasized that management and personnel 'undertake to draw opportunities for training and promotion to the attention of all eligible employees and inform employees of this agreement on equal opportunities' (TUC, 1981: 9). The details of the Charter are important because they illustrate a new level of commitment on the part of the TUC to equal opportunities. The Charter also recognized that trade unions have a unique responsibility (and potential) to pursue and deliver a serious programme of equal opportunities.

Increasingly, during the mid-1980s and early 1990s, individual trade unions, including NATFHE and, to a lesser extent, the AUT, have, at national and regional levels, established separate advisory committees, co-opting systems, reserved seats and other structures to work on race, gender and equal opportunity issues and have adopted equal opportunity statements and often an array of accompanying policies. Some unions, for example the Transport and General Workers Union and NATFHE, have appointed national equal opportunities officials (Wrench, 1992; Virdee and Grint, 1994).

The assessments of the effects of these shifts in trade union approaches to equality issues show limited success (GLC, 1984; Lee, 1984; Lancashire Association of Trades Councils, 1985). In 1988, the TUC's survey of twenty-four unions found that there was little evidence of adoption by unions of rules against racist behaviour and that there was little change in the numbers of black officials at higher levels in union structures. Significantly, the survey found that only a small minority of unions accepted the principle of official structures for black members' self-organization (*Labour Research*, July, 1988). Virdee and Grint (1994: 207–8) have argued that 'almost [no unions], with the primary exception of NALGO [National Association of Local Government Officers], have experienced the growth of self-organised black and minority groups along the lines rather more common for women members'. Union hostility to black self-organization can be interpreted in part as a continued adherence to the idea of a unified working class and the tenacity of labour's relegation of race as a secondary issue to class. However, the point that Virdee and Grint raise above in relation to women trade unionists is important. Women's self-organization within individual trade unions is, if not welcomed, tolerated. This willingness to 'tolerate' women's self-organization appears immediately to contradict this 'divisive' argument. The different approaches to the issues of gender and race within the trade union movement and labourist politics more broadly also reflect the greater degree of acceptability that gender has within the equal opportunities rubric (see Chapters 4 and 5 for a more detailed discussion of this). Black self-organization in trade unions symbolizes black political mobilization and lends those unions black political images. It is the potential of black self-organization to represent a new political agenda (which focuses on issues outside of a traditional labourist agenda) that concerns trade unions (cf. debates around Black Sections in the Labour Party; Knowles, 1992: 151–63; Solomos and Back, 1995).

While many black workers/trade unionists feel that the way to get their voices heard is through self-organization within unions, union hierarchies continue to prefer a model of 'passive assimilation', whereby minorities rise through the ranks of the union movement through traditional routes and provide role models for others to follow (Virdee and Grint, 1994).

This approach persists despite the clear evidence of low participation rates of black trade union members (Runnymede Trust, 1974; Lee, 1984; Lancashire Association of Trades Councils, 1985; *Labour Research,* July, 1988; CRE, 1992). Even without this body of writing and research, 'just a cursory glance at the composition of union conferences, their regional or national executive bodies, their TUC Congress delegations or their full-time office post holders, shows an underrepresentation of ethnic minority members' (CRE, 1992: 7). What appears to be a significant policy–practice gap has been noted by other commentators. In their study of ethnic minorities and employment practice in six organizations, Jewson *et al.* (1990: 181) found:

> In most cases there appeared to be little evidence of trade unions at our research sites having taken initiatives with respect to ethnic minority employment . . . in the majority of cases it appeared that trade unions had principally responded to management initiatives. They had been re-active rather than pro-active.

These researchers also discovered that:

> Most trade union representatives interviewed had relatively little knowledge or expertise in the area of equal opportunities. Most were unable to say whether their own trade unions had equal opportunities policies or recommended clauses for incorporation into agreements.
>
> (Jewson *et al.*, 1990: 182)

The discrepancy between nationally formulated equality policies and local knowledge/activity also raises broader questions as to the ability of top-down models of equal opportunities to execute a successful programme of equality-orientated action at a local level (see Chapters 5 and 6). While there have obviously been shifts in the response of the trade union movement to black and minority workers since the 1950s, it would appear that in the 1990s trade unions have only progressed to a position in which they 'are not essentially exclusivist nor inherently racist ... trade unions are therefore neither unambiguously advantageous nor disadvantageous for blacks and minorities' (Virdee and Grint, 1994: 222). Chapter 6 examines the nature of this ambiguous relationship in terms of the local activities and responses to equality issues of NATFHE and the AUT in the four university case studies. What I now explore are the national 'faces' of these two unions and the concept of higher education containing a unionized workforce.

Academic trade unionism

A note on the white collar trade union debate

As the AUT and NATFHE are professional trade unions, this section of the chapter provides a (brief) overview of the theoretical approaches used to examine the political character of professional trade unions. Despite the over-simplification that the middle classes can be measured by their commitment to individualism (anti-unionism) and the working classes to collectivism (pro-unionism), the extensive establishment of white collar trade unionism has presented a sufficient degree of *contradiction* to generate a long-running and divided academic debate. This debate has tended to be collapsed into the dichotomy of whether white collar unionism represents the proletarianization of the middle/professional classes (Lockwood, 1958; Prandy, 1965; Blackburn, 1967; Crompton, 1976; Prandy *et al.*, 1983), or whether white collar unionism represents pragmatic attempts by middle/professional class workers to retain/gain control and influence in the capital/managerial function of the labour processes (Bain, 1967, 1972; Weir, 1976).

As Carter (1985) notes these two positions can be identified as the 'sociological approach' (which focuses on the *character* of white collar trade unionism and attempts to connect it with social class) and the 'industrial relations approach' (which focuses on the *growth* of white collar trade unionism and denies any firm relationship with social class). For example, Bain (1967, 1972), whose work is most commonly associated with the industrial relations approach, argues that white collar workers join trade unions primarily 'to control more effectively their work situation'. Bain (1972: 188) saw an increasing necessity for white collar workers to belong to trade unions as white collar employment became 'more concentrated and bureaucratised and individual white collar workers find that they have less and less ability to influence the making and the administration of rules by which they are governed on the job'. For Bain, the interests of white collar workers could be directly aligned with those of management.

In contrast to the industrial relations perspective, the neo-Weberian sociological perspectives (Lockwood, 1958; Prandy, 1965; Blackburn, 1967; Prandy *et al.*, 1983) sought to make links between status, class and unionization. Lockwood (1958) argued that increasing bureaucratization broke down old employer/employee individualism and acted as a primary factor in the growth of clerical unionization.

Both Prandy (1965) and Blackburn (1967) sought to build on Lockwood's work. Prandy's study of engineering technicians claimed it was loss of authority in the workplace and factors such as low pay which lay behind the development of a 'class view' of the employment relationship and its expression in the form of unionization. For Blackburn, it was a union's image and its recruitment policies that were essential elements to white collar union growth (Carter, 1985).

In attempting briefly to map out some of the main contours of what is now a rather dated debate, it is the polarization of the industrial relations and sociological themes that appears to need questioning. Rather than view the growth and character of white collar trade unions as exclusive to one or the other, it is clearly possible to see the two as interrelated. That there is a degree of convergence between the two positions is an argument which I apply in my consideration of academic unionism.

Profiling the AUT and NATFHE

Given the above debate, one of the obvious questions which this section of the chapter seeks to address is: Does academic unionization represent a strategy by academics to maintain influence over their workplace or do they represent a collective strategy to defend their labour against university management? I will suggest below that the AUT and NATFHE represent both of these positions to a greater or lesser extent (see Chapter 6).

The AUT
The AUT represents the 'old' university sector. Its claimed membership at the end of 1990 was around 32,000. This membership is drawn vertically from academic hierarchies but also includes academic-related staff (administrators, librarians and computer support staff). This latter grouping makes up 40 per cent of the total (Farnham, 1991). Vice-chancellors, principals and other senior managers/administrators are eligible for full membership of the AUT. The AUT has a predominantly male membership profile (85 per cent of its total). At the time of the research the union does not collect data relating to the ethnicity profile of its membership. The AUT recruits from all regions of Britain and Northern Ireland. The AUT has a fairly heterogeneous membership despite drawing its membership from a single sector

of higher education. The AUT has only a relatively small membership base with a potential membership of 52,000. Its highest recorded membership was in the early 1980s at around 34,000. Since this peak, membership has stabilized at around 32,000 (Farnham, 1991).

Founded in 1919 as a staff association, the AUT has functioned for the greater part of its history as a professional association, finally affiliating to the TUC in 1976 after a protracted debate and two national ballots. While Garabino and Aussieker (1975) argued that as far back as 1969 the AUT had made the transition to being a union, Williams *et al.* (1974) concluded from their research that most university teachers belonging to the AUT did not regard themselves as union members. In 1971, the first vote as to whether to affiliate to the TUC was defeated by a 65 per cent to 35 per cent margin and, in 1976, when the second vote was taken, there was a 58 per cent to 42 per cent split in favour of affiliation. The themes of the debate that took place, often in the *AUT Bulletin*, between these votes provide an insight into how the AUT membership perceived both itself and trade unionism (Garabino and Aussieker, 1975). In 1971, the AUT leadership was against affiliation. In the March 1971 *AUT Bulletin* of that year, AUT officials argued that the AUT's fundamental ethic 'is universalist, progressive, egalitarian and humane . . . the AUT is concerned primarily with non-material objectives and its stance is not based on an assumption of permanent conflict' (p. 21). Such arguments appeared to indicate a fear that formal association with the trade union movement would push the AUT into confrontational and adversarial relationships with universities and that professional (middle-class) concerns would be subsumed to economic (working-class) concerns.

Affiliation to the TUC in 1976 has not resolved the AUT's professional/union dichotomy. The contemporary character of the AUT remains ambivalent, blurring its identity between the two. In its 'statements of purpose', the AUT describes itself as representing the full range of work and professional concerns of its members, 'the main objective of AUT policy is to secure the full participation of all academic related staff in the government of their institutions' (AUT, 1988: 1), although it proceeds to concede to the Academic Senate 'all decision-making on purely academic matters' (ibid., p. 3). Yet in its *Rules of Association*, the AUT makes the more robust, 'union-orientated' statement that the 'objects of the Association shall be the advancement of University Education and Research, the regulation of relations between University Teachers and their employers, the *promotion of common action by University Teachers* and the safe-guarding of the interests of the members' (AUT, 1989: 1; emphasis added). The ambiguous professional association/trade union identity of the AUT continually surfaced in the fieldwork and is explored in Chapter 6.

NATFHE
Unlike the AUT, NATFHE has a much more recent history and although it calls itself an association, an 'easier' trade union identity. NATFHE was formed in 1976 by a merger between the Association of Teachers in Technical

Institutions and the Association of Teachers in Departments and Colleges of Education. Organized in fourteen regions and eight hundred branches, NATFHE's membership base is extensive. NATFHE has had an increasing membership throughout the 1980s, reaching an estimated 82,000 in 1988, but this has since fallen and stabilized at around 72,000 in 1993 (NATFHE estimates, 1993). NATFHE recruits its membership across the 'new' university and the further education sectors. NATFHE limits its membership mainly to teachers in either sector and although its membership base is much wider than the AUT, the overwhelming teacher membership gives NATFHE a more homogeneous profile. However, the diversity of the higher and further education contexts from which NATFHE recruits its membership means that the apparent homogeneity is diluted – the employment and professional interests of higher and further education lecturers are not necessarily synonymous. It is estimated that NATFHE's membership is divided between some 18,000 (one in four) members in the 'new university' sector, with the rest being in further education, which includes those in agricultural education, adult education and penal education. These figures (Farnham, 1991) clearly demonstrate that higher education NATFHE members represent a distinct, if substantial, minority. Unlike the AUT, NATFHE has a much larger female membership – about one-third of the total membership. Although it does not monitor its members' ethnicity, it is estimated at around 2 per cent, undoubtedly much larger than the total of the AUT's black and other minority ethnic membership (ibid.).

Unlike the AUT's position in the 'old university' sector, NATFHE's position is, in theory, exposed, in terms of membership, to competition via the existence of the Association of Polytechnic and College Teachers (APCT). However, as Farnham (1991) notes the APCT (created in 1973 as a union for polytechnic staff) is too small and peripheral (it has a membership of around 3000) to represent any serious challenge to NATFHE.

Although NATFHE differs in many respects from the AUT in terms of longevity, history, membership, size, job territory and structure (NATFHE operates at a regional level), its stated functions as a higher (and further) education trade union – protecting members' interests and the profession – have a similar echo to those made by the AUT. For example, the NATFHE *Members Handbook* states: 'NATFHE is organised and staffed to promote the educational and professional concerns of members and their employment interests . . . belonging to NATFHE gives you important protection and excellent services' (NATFHE, 1993: 4).

It is NATFHE's character as a union which has been forged in a very different context to the AUT (i.e. the public sector), which provides one of the most crucial differences between the two unions. Public sector unionism has been commented on for its high rate of union membership and for its apparent commitment to the ethics of the trade union movement (Blyton *et al.*, 1981; Prandy *et al.*, 1983; Virdee and Grint, 1994), which often overlaps into (non-official) support for the Labour Party. To what extent, then, were the differences between the AUT and NATFHE reflected in their national responses to equal opportunities questions and their related equal opportunities structures?

AUT: *national equality structures*

During the period of my research, the AUT had what can best be described as a minimalist national equal opportunities structure. This comprised a Women's Committee (formed in 1983) and an Equal Opportunities Working Party (formed in 1988 and by being a working party has a finite life). The brief of the latter incorporated issues of 'race', disability, age, sexuality and other aspects of equal opportunities which were not seen as directly relating to gender. The Women's Committee and the Equal Opportunities Working Party acted in an advisory capacity to the National Executive Committee (NEC) of the AUT which, in turn, reported to the Governing Council of the AUT. In other words, they had limited powers. The membership of these committees was not directly elected but made up of twenty-four (elected) members of the NEC who then sat on two of the six advisory committees. The Women's Committee meets four times a year and organizes the annual one-day AUT conference for its women members. The Equal Opportunities Working Party, which certainly appeared peripheral to the AUT's broader organizational structure, did not meet while I was conducting the fieldwork and had not actually met for the eighteen months preceding my research and its existence was being questioned. The AUT has no national official with a specific brief for equal opportunities work. Equality-related work and responsibilities had been incorporated into the already broad portfolio of the assistant general secretary (the post includes negotiation and carries the AUT's education, international and European brief). The most visible nationally based evidence of the AUT's equal opportunities policy is the triennial newsletter, *AUT Woman*, which was launched in 1983 and is circulated to all members of the AUT.

NATFHE: *national equality structures*

In contrast, NATFHE has a developed, if uneven, national equal opportunities structure. Since 1982, it has had an Equal Opportunities Committee which advises the National Executive and meets between three and four times a year. The Equal Opportunities Committee is itself serviced by two advisory committees: the Racial Equality Standing Committee[1] and the Women's Rights Standing Committee, both of which meet four or more times a year and are made up of the (elected) members of the Equal Opportunity Committee. In an effort to streamline these structures, a part-time post of national equal opportunities adviser was created in 1993, a post which is directly responsible to the general secretary. This structural system of an overall equal opportunities committee with two specialized sub-committees is supposed to be repeated in the fourteen regions, although this is not enforced and has only been taken up by the regions on an *ad hoc* basis (*NATFHE Journal*, Autumn, 1993). Since the mid-1980s, the National Executive Committee has reserved places for women and black members as part of its positive action strategy for increasing the participation of these groups. Most visibly, NATFHE elected, during the research, a black woman president, although to what extent this can actually be taken as a reliable indicator of an organization's equality ethos is uncertain. However, that there is an active black NATFHE membership was also indicated by the presence of a NATFHE representative on the TUC Race Relations Advisory Committee and the NATFHE delegation which attended the 1993 TUC Black Workers Conference. This delegation presented a motion demanding the creation of three further places for black members on the TUC General Council (*NATFHE Journal*, Autumn, 1993).[2]

Like the AUT, NATFHE has an annual one-day conference for its women members but it also has annual one-day conferences for its black members and more recently for its lesbian and gay members. Unlike the AUT, which only works with the CRE and the Equal Opportunities Commission, NATFHE is in contact with political organizations outside of its immediate territory – it is affiliated to both the Anti-Racist Alliance and the Anti-Nazi League.

While this outline of national equal opportunity structures provides a 'shop window' on the AUT's and NATFHE's responses to equality issues, what I wish to explore in the final part of this chapter is to what extent the academic membership of the AUT and NATFHE possesses a political consciousness which is sympathetic to the equal opportunities agenda. While there is evidence that the national face of both the AUT and NATFHE does contain an equal opportunities dimension, it is important to examine whether this reflects the shared values of the AUT's and NATFHE's membership (i.e. academics). Analysis of the trade union movement has highlighted gaps between the official union political values/approaches and the political values of rank and file members (see, for example, Miles and Phizacklea, 1977; J. Kelly, 1988; see also Chapter 6, where I discuss whether equal opportunities activists perceive their unions as forums which support equal opportunities issues).

The nature of academic political consciousness

The equal opportunities agenda is dominated by the (seemingly) 'non-class' issues of gender, race, disability and sexuality, and is linked to such other political concerns as environmentalism and peace movements. Support for these issues has been predominantly associated with certain radicalized sections of the middle class – mainly welfare professionals but also media/ arts workers and, significantly, academics (Parkin, 1968).

As Bonnet (1993) notes theoretical approaches to the analysis of middle-class radicalism have been divided between those approaches which argue that the radicalized faction of the middle classes have replaced the working classes as the main opponents of capitalism (Mallet, 1968; Gouldner, 1979) and those approaches which argue that middle-class radicalism has developed in conjunction with existing working-class political activism (Parkin, 1968; Roberts *et al.*, 1977).

Bonnet critically examines how explanations of middle-class radicalism tend to focus on objective causes: higher education, low economic reward and a 'semi-autonomous' location in the capitalist economy. It is significant that higher education is identified as playing a key role in the radicalization process. For example, both Parkin (1968) and Gouldner (1979) argue that it is within a (politically liberating) system of higher education that an anti-authority 'culture of critical discourse' is developed and promoted. Similarly, Roberts *et al.* (1977: 146) urge that 'anyone wishing to find support for political ideologies to the left of Labour . . . is better advised to visit a university than a trade union branch meeting'.

Having absorbed the 'culture of critical discourse' via the higher education experience, the radicalization process continues because of the tendency of a faction of the middle class to enter occupations which have low economic rewards (and status). The radicalization process is then consolidated by the occupational locations of these occupations. They are often in areas dislocated, or seemingly (semi)autonomous, from the immediate capitalist economy, for example the welfare sector, education (including higher education), and creative professions (Cotgrove and Duff, 1980).

Applying these radicalizing criteria to academics would clearly place them within the radicalized faction of the middle class. Academics (sociologists in particular) have been consistently targeted by the New Right as 'responsible for the ascendancy of permissive values' (*The Guardian*, 19 January 1993), they can be identified as semi-autonomous employees and surveys of academics' political party allegiances show increasing support for the Labour Party (Halsey and Trow, 1971; Williams *et al.*, 1974; Halsey, 1992). However, not only do the causes of radicalization arguments tend to be overly deterministic and overstate the liberalizing/radicalizing effects of higher education, but they also avoid an analysis of the *contradictions* of the concept of a radicalized middle class (Bonnet, 1993; see also Offe, 1984 and Mattausch, 1989).

While the immediate contradictions which underpin the position of 'frontline' public sector professionals may not take exactly the same form regarding the position of academics, academics do occupy a contradictory and shadowy location within the capitalist state. There is a complex tension between higher education as a site in which a culture of critical or oppositional discourse is produced and higher education as a site in which state-sponsored discourses and oppressive state activities appear to be legitimized. For example, Halsey (1992) claims that a 'long tradition of social criticism . . . has existed in British universities' (pp. 248–9) and that 'university teachers generally are politically much more to the left than the non-university middle class; their profile of party allegiance resembles more that of the manual working class' (p. 256). Yet there is an inherent difficulty in reconciling these claims with Gutzmore's (1983: 27) argument, that 'it is difficult even to begin to distinguish between the function in the class struggle in Britain of those, on the one hand, whose role is openly that of repression and those, on the other, whose ostensible role is that of objective academic research'.

In attempting to theorize this tension, Wright (1979) has argued that the bourgeois class needs academic production, it needs scientific research and it needs imaginative reformulations of bourgeois ideology. However, this production needs a certain level of autonomy to be effective. This autonomy, in the form of 'academic freedom', has successfully created an image of open and free discussion which is so essential for bourgeois liberalist ideology, but it has simultaneously created a greater space for ideas which can challenge bourgeois ideology. It is this autonomy which makes the role of academics complex and contradictory – that is, this role can be oppositional and critical or it can be in the interests of the state.

Quoting from Keynes, that 'madmen in authority, who hear voices in the air, are distilling their frenzy from some academic scribbler of a few years back', Bulmer (1986: 12) has argued that the relationship between academics, their research project and the political project of the state, is forged through processes of gradual and selective permeation rather than being functional. However, 'knowledge producers are set in social milieus' (Goldberg, 1993: 149), and while this relationship may not always be crude and obvious (nor is it necessarily all-encompassing), the *potential* for academics to service the interests of the state remains. As Solomos (1989: 5) notes:

> Whatever the academic argument in favour of doing a specific piece of research it is politically naive and potentially dangerous to see research as autonomous from its contextual political environment and governments and other interested groups necessarily take a strong role and have a stake in academic research about so-called deviants in society.

Historically, social research into the area of race has provided one of the clearest examples of the fusion between academic production and the interests of various state agencies (Bourne, 1980; Gilroy, 1980; Lawrence, 1981, 1982; Gutzmore, 1983; Goldberg, 1993).

It would be a mistake, then, to expect academics to possess a homogeneous political consciousness which is committed to issues of social justice and equal opportunities. Their concern with such political questions can be characterized by contradiction and ambiguity. On the one hand, academics share the characteristics of the radicalized faction of the middle classes and the related notions of progressive political thinking, yet on the other, academics may subscribe to a middle-class ideology which is dominated by such concerns as individualism, careerism and competitiveness (increasingly so within the market-orientated shifts in higher education) and academics may be engaged in the production of knowledge which the state is able to use to legitimize its own discourses and activities.

Conclusion

This chapter has sought to connect three focal concerns: the responses of the trade union movement to black workers and equality issues; the character and background of the AUT and NATFHE and these unions' specific responses to equal opportunities; and the nature and orientation of academic political consciousness. The chapter has argued that while the trade union movement has shifted its position from its colour-blind approaches, this shift has resulted in largely symbolic measures to address issues of racial inequality that have failed to impact at the local level of union activity. While the AUT and NATFHE have participated in this general shift and established forms of a national equal opportunities structure, the extent of the policy/practice gap at the local level will be explored in Chapter 6. This chapter has argued that the AUT in particular has had a historical ambiguity about being linked to trade union politics and while NATFHE may be more comfortable with these political associations, this is a result of its members being formerly employed in the public sector and this may be subject to change as it loses its public sector roots. I have explored the question of whether academics can be expected to be more sympathetic to the non-class concerns of the equal opportunities agenda through their association with the radicalized faction of the middle classes. However, the contradictions and ambiguities involved in the role of academics in a capitalist organized society means that it would be incorrect to expect academics, and academic institutions to have a higher than average degree of commitment and subscription to equal opportunities discourses.

4

Analysing Equal Opportunities
Policy Documents

Introduction

While the terms 'equal opportunities' and, to a lesser extent, 'anti-racism' have gained much currency over the last decade, the political and theoretical concepts which lie behind these terms are often conflicting. This conflict in interpretation tends to centre around the apparent dichotomy of equal opportunities models which aim for either 'equal treatment' or 'equal shares' (Young, 1989), 'fair chance' or 'fair outcome' (Cockburn, 1992). Jewson and Mason (1986) have argued that the competing understandings of equal opportunities can be summarized as 'liberal' and 'radical'. Within the liberal model of equal opportunities the concepts of 'fairness' and 'non-discrimination' play a key role: '[Equality] policy makers are required to ensure that the rules of the competition are not discriminatory and that they are fairly enforced on all' (Jewson and Mason, 1986: 313). However, within the radical model of equal opportunities it is the (more politicized) concepts of redistribution and justice which are of central concern: 'Neither fair procedures nor the operation of the market are of inherent interest to radicals. What matters is whether these or any other mechanisms, deliver the goods' (Mason, 1990: 51). The radical model of equal opportunities, then, emphasizes the 'delivery of goods' or equality of outcome. In practice, this is measured by the representativeness of previously excluded groups. While the liberal and radical models may both follow similar positive action policy procedures, it is its longer-term aim of altering patterns of recruitment or resource allocation which principally distinguishes the radical from the liberal interpretation of equal opportunities. As Young (1992) notes, either model can operate successfully if its aims are clear and there is consensus around those aims. However clarity and agreement around equal opportunities are infrequent: 'Either understanding, if explicit and shared, can provide a coherent basis for policy. But such explicitness is rare and the coexistence of contrasting understandings within the same organisation more common' (p. 261). Drawing on these arguments, the following chapters analyse the research data in order to explore the differing 'appreciative contexts' (Young, 1992) of equal opportunities policy formation and implementation in higher education.

This chapter considers the equal opportunities policy documentation that was made available to me by each of the case-study universities. The policy documentation represents the formal position which institutions have taken up in relation to equal opportunities issues. Equal opportunities policies texts are, then, the 'frontline' or the public face of an institution's approach to, and interpretation of, equal opportunities – in all my early visits to the case-studies universities, I was immediately provided with a number of equal opportunities related documentation. For these reasons, it is important to give a reading of this presentational data (Farish *et al.*, 1995). The first part of the chapter explores what the documentation claimed/stated, what issues the documentation covered and what were the areas of commonality and diversity. Given that the concept and term 'equal opportunities' dominates the policy documents, the second part of the chapter focuses on the interpretations that senior management and equal opportunities policy-makers and implementators gave the concept and asks to what extent equal opportunities documentation can be seen as part of an institution's public relations strategies.

Equal opportunities policy texts

Although it varied in amount and appearance – from glossy booklets to single-page statements to lengthy discussion papers – all the case-study universities had some form of equal opportunities documentation. There was also variation in authorship of the documentation and the audience at which it was aimed. For example, Castlebrook University had its entire equal opportunities policies contained in a glossy publicity booklet which bore the signature of the pro-vice-chancellor, implying senior management authorship. Yet at Russell College, the documentation was fragmented and appeared to be anonymous. While such variations obviously reflect wider differences in the institutions' approaches to equal opportunities, there were areas of standardization in terms of the issues that institutions had developed policy around. All four case studies had documentation relating to three main areas: each had a formal equal opportunities statement; each had sexual and racial harassment policies; and each had policies relating to academic affairs, an area which covered a range of issues from student recruitment to curriculum content to staff recruitment.

While I set out below the content and themes of the equal opportunities policy texts in these areas, what I want to emphasize is both their variation, mainly in the language used, and their standardization, mainly in terms of the use of the concepts of anti-discrimination and fairness. In other words, differences did exist in the policy texts but these differences occurred within the well-defined limits of a converged liberal-radical equal opportunities discourse (Ball, 1994).

Equal opportunities statement of policies

All four case-study universities had a statement or declaration, usually just a few paragraphs in length, of their equal opportunities policy commitments. These statements are important because they not only summarize the thrust of the universities' approach to, and basis of, their equal opportunities policy, but they are often the most visible and widely disseminated aspect of an organization's equal opportunity policy. For example, it is the equal opportunities policy statement which will appear in the university prospectus (see Jewson *et al.*, 1991, 1993) and which will also be included in employment application forms, student and staff packs and publicity material.

All the statements referred to their commitment not to discriminate on the grounds of various social categories: gender, race, nationality, marital status, age, disability and dependants. However, there were variations in the categories listed. For example, Russell College made no mention of sexual orientation.[1] Northfield and Peoples Universities clearly stated an ethical context to their anti-discriminatory commitments. Northfield University claimed that its intention was to 'pursue not only the letter of the law but also *the spirit* of the law' (emphasis added). Peoples University stated that 'in addition to being unjust, all forms of discrimination represent a waste of human resources and a denial of the opportunity for individual self-fulfilment'. Castlebrook University clearly implied a retention of a commitment to one of the original roles of the polytechnics (i.e. of providing an educational service to the local community): 'as an institution based in a deprived inner city area it will establish and maintain close links with the local community and will seek to extend employment and educational opportunities for local people'. Two of the case-study universities offered an open commitment to following programmes of positive action to achieve representation. Northfield University declared an intention to 'ensure an equitable gender balance and appropriate representation of minority ethnic groups and people with disability', while Peoples University similarly declared that its aim was to 'increase the level of participation of students, staff and clients of those groups that are currently under-represented'.

It was in the statements of the two 'new' universities that the only references to equal opportunities training were made. While for Northfield University this appeared only to apply to those who were, or would be, involved in the selection and recruitment of staff and students, Castlebrook University claimed that 'equal opportunity training will be provided for *all* employees' (emphasis added).

Significantly, of the four policy statements, only those of the two 'old' universities made explicit reference to treating candidates on the basis of their individual merit and ability alone as part of their equal opportunities policies (see Chapter 2).

Despite the relative brevity of these statements of commitment to equal opportunities, a number of converged and contradictory policy aims emerge. While all four universities declare their anti-discriminatory (liberal) intentions, two (Northfield and Peoples Universities) combine this with the (radical) aim of increasing representation and two (Russell College and Peoples University) combine this with the (traditional) aim of discriminating only on the basis of merit and ability. It is highly significant that convergence/ confusion and ambiguity can be seen in these statements which represent the policy basis of an institution's stance on equal opportunities.

Sexual and racial harassment policies

All four case studies had racial and sexual harassment codes. Castlebrook University had a third harassment code relating to sexual preference and Northfield University incorporated harassment relating to sexuality into its sexual harassment code of practice. Harassment codes have become an integral part of equal opportunities policies. In effect, they have come to represent the *penal* aspect of the policies and as such can become one of the most contentious elements of an equal opportunities programme, especially as they aim to impact directly on the behaviour of individuals within the institution. Like statements of commitment, harassment codes also tend to be a very public part of an organization's equal opportunities programme in that they are widely distributed to all employees and students via inclusion in handbooks and induction packages. The harassment codes were the most standardized policy documents, reading as if written to the same formula. All the harassment codes offered very similar definitions of sexual and racial harassment and provided examples of behaviour which would constitute such harassment. In terms of sexual harassment, these examples ranged from leering, invasion of personal space, displays of pornographic material to verbal or physical assault. In terms of racial harassment, the given examples ranged from derogatory name calling, racist jokes, racist verbal and written comments, displays of racist material to making threats and assault. All four universities cited the Sex Discrimination Act (1975) and the Race Relations Act (1976) as the context of their harassment codes. The emphasis on legislation can be seen as part of contentiousness of harassment codes. It acts to extend the penal aspect of the harassment policies but it also acts to legitimize the policies (i.e. distance them from 'political correctness'). Each of the harassment codes had detailed steps about what a student or member of staff should do should they be sexually or racially harassed and the procedures which would follow. For example, Northfield University's harassment code explained how a complaint could be taken straight to the director who would take action immediately which could include the relocation of the harasser if necessary. Additionally, the university gave details of the appointment and role of a sexual harassment officer. The statement emphasized how anyone seeking advice, making a complaint or assisting in an investigation would be offered support and protected against victimization or discrimination. It is significant that Northfield University's harassment code was the only one to include a clause relating to false allegations: 'making a *false allegation* with *malicious intent* may result in the disciplinary code being invoked' (*Sexual Harassment Policy Statement*, 1990), thus raising as it inevitably does the spectre of women lying about sexual abuse.

The harassment codes of Peoples University and Russell College were very similar and the most detailed of the four codes in terms of their complaints procedures. All the harassment codes made reference to supporting a complainant and ensuring that a complainant would be protected from retaliation or further victimization, yet there was no detail as to how this may be ensured or the nature of the support that should be offered. Peoples University did note the benefits of counselling but, significantly, only mentioned this in relation to the offender/harasser: 'The University regards the use of expert counselling about harassment as of positive benefit and arrangements will be made for such counselling for all offenders who indicate that they would find it helpful' (*Dealing With Sexual and Racial Harassment: A Code of Practice*, 1991: 7).

The case studies' harassment policies were cautious documents. They appeared to have a dual aim of attempting to reassure a hostile and suspicious audience and to reassure those audiences whom harassment is most likely to affect. This inevitably places constraints on the effectiveness of the codes, reassuring neither audience. The limitations of all the case studies' harassment policies can be seen in their very standardization. For example, while all of the universities' codes listed categories of what constituted harassing behaviour, none of the codes recognized that such behaviour does not necessarily fall into one neat category. As L. Kelly (1988: 48) has argued in relation to sexual abuse and violence against women:

> There are no clearly defined and discrete analytical categories into which women's experiences can be placed. The experiences women have and how they are subjectively defined shade into and out of a given category such as sexual harassment, which includes looks, gestures and remarks as well as acts which may be defined as assault or rape.

Similarly, racial harassment codes cannot provide 'protection' for black people from seemingly race-neutral or coded language or events (see Chapter 1). They are only designed to cope with such obvious categories as racist jokes, racist material and racial abuse. In the absence of this recognition, the harassment codes of the four case studies appeared in a technicist and rationalist vacuum. They did not deal with racism or sexism in the organization *per se*, but only with the racialized or gendered victimization of individuals. None of the codes examined in this research made any reference to, let alone provisions for, responding to experiences of racism and/or sexism outside of the victimization paradigm. Northfield University came the closest to attempting a broader approach to the issue of sexual harassment by creating the post of sexual harassment officer, whose brief not only included casework but also involved wider strategies of raising awareness and training regarding sexual harassment. Yet, as I shall discuss later, it was in Northfield University where there was the greatest degree of hostility to harassment initiatives.

Policies on equal opportunities in academic affairs

This was the third area in which all the case-study universities had some form of documentation. Again this varied in its amount and its visual appearance. Castlebrook University had the most glossily packaged documentation, Peoples University the most extensive, Northfield University was in the process of redrafting their documentation, and Russell College had the least developed policies. The documentation in this category, covered three areas: student recruitment and admissions; curriculum content, teaching and course assessment; and staff recruitment, training and development. Despite the presence of the third category, these policies tended to be more heavily weighted towards equal opportunities and the student, rather than the staff, body within the case studies. In all four universities, the equal opportunities policies in academic affairs formed the core of their overall equal opportunities programmes, building on the claims of their equal opportunities policy statements. For example, at Castlebrook University, equal opportunities in academic affairs appeared within the main equal opportunities document *Making Equal Opportunities Work* (1993), and in Peoples University, equal opportunities in academic affairs appeared as an integral part of their five-year *Equal Opportunities Action Plan* devised in 1990:

> The University wishes to ensure that prior experiences and learning are duly valued, that the curriculum reflects the diversity of cultural experiences in society and that all processes associated with recruitment, admission, teaching and learning, progression and assessment are consistent with the provision of equal opportunities.
> (*University's Views on Equal Opportunities in Academic Affairs*, 1991: 1)

However, the policy documents relating to equal opportunities in academic affairs tended to be more hidden and far less widely disseminated or 'known' about in the wider institution. In other words, the profile of these documents was much lower than the equal opportunities statement for the harassment codes. Although I do not intend an extensive rehearsal of the details of the equal opportunities in academic affairs documentation, I outline below the key themes of these policies.

Student recruitment and admissions

Significantly, student recruitment was an area in which all the case-study universities placed an emphasis not on anti-discriminatory practice, but on the need for *representation* in relation to gender, ethnicity, class, age and disability. Northfield, Castlebrook and Peoples Universities all underlined their commitment to providing access to courses to students without a traditional (three 'A' level) profile. Castlebrook University noted its commitment to increasing and improving routes of access for such students and highlighted strategies for achieving this: greater diversity in course structure, extension of short course, part-time and evening provision, and the modularization of courses to create more flexible learning opportunities, including interdisciplinary initiatives. Castlebrook University further stated, that where particular groups were under-represented on courses, the university would seek to identify the cause of this and take positive action to address the issues responsible for such under-representation (*Making Equal Opportunities Work*, 1993: 8).

Peoples University declared itself committed to a 10 per cent increase in the number of registered students with low qualifications (i.e. below 'A' level), by 1995 and emphasized that first attention would be paid to recruiting black and minority ethnic students on all courses and recruiting women in maths, science and technology courses (*Equal Opportunities Action Plan*, 1990: 1). Echoing this, Northfield University stated that 'prior learning and experience of students will be recognised alongside other forms of qualification for admission and progression to programmes of study' (*Equal Opportunities in Academic Affairs: A Policy Statement*, 1989: 2). Russell College made a number of recommendations in relation to the recruitment and admission of black and minority ethnic students. These ranged from the need to review the college's publicity material and selective advertising, to the evaluation of interviewing practices and selection criteria and the establishment of access courses (*Report from the University's Central Academic Board*, 1986: 7–8). All four case-study universities emphasized their commitment to providing a physical environment which would improve the representation of students with disabilities.

Student recruitment was an area in which the policy statements shared a consensus around the more radical equal opportunities aim of representation. However, there was a significant lack of reference to student experiences once within the institution (see Bird, 1996).

Curriculum content and development

Reflecting the consensus regarding student representation was the degree of commonality in the policy statements relating to teaching and learning. The policy recommendations of all four case studies focused on the need for teaching, learning and assessment strategies to incorporate equal opportunities dimensions and reflect cultural diversity and gender experiences in curriculum content. Peoples University and Castlebrook University had the most extensive policy coverage in this area. For example, Peoples University urged that all academic units encourage a climate of discussion on equal opportunities, that course design and planning should involve a thorough and monitored consideration of equal opportunities issues, and that the university should encourage the development of courses which have as their focus issues of equal opportunities or discrimination. The university had developed an *Equal Opportunities Guidelines in Course Material* booklet, which had as its central concern the production of an academic curriculum which adequately and 'fairly' represented (and was relevant to) women, black and minority ethnic communities, people with disabilities, lesbians and gay men, and working-class people.[2]

The most politicized of the policy texts in this area came from Castlebrook University. For example, the university claimed, 'it is implicit in this curriculum development policy that reversing negative attitudes towards disadvantaged groups of students, or individuals, is a legitimate educational aim which should permeate all areas of the curriculum and become integral to the educational process' (*Making Equal Opportunities Work*, 1993: 9). The document continued to state that all course materials would be subject to scrutiny and revision to avoid any discriminatory terminology, information and concepts and that courses should reflect cultural diversity and incorporate perspectives which are 'neither Eurocentric nor male-dominated' (ibid.). The document urged that, in subject areas where the numbers of women students have traditionally been low, consideration be given to teaching women separately as a way of overcoming historical stereotyping and to enable the learning of non-traditional skills. The Castlebrook University document placed an emphasis on the necessity of a holistic learning environment in which 'all students are given the opportunity to realise their full potential' (p. 10), and built on this emphasis by stating the need to consider the effectiveness of different teaching methods and to vary the modes of course assessment. The document also noted that adequate nursery provision was an essential element of increasing access to higher education for non-traditional students, particularly women, stating that the university is 'committed to maintaining and developing current nursery provision' (ibid.). Related to this, the *Making Equal Opportunities Work* document stated its recognition of the home responsibilities of students and the impact these can have on the ability for attendance. It urged course directors and heads of schools to bear this in mind when timetabling and for the need to adopt a flexible approach to this.[3]

The policy documents in all four case studies also referenced the need for student facilities – halls of residence, libraries, canteens – and pastoral and advisory services to incorporate an equal opportunities dimension and in particular emphasized their commitment to ensuring access for students with disabilities.

The case study documentation in relation to teaching and curriculum content was steeped in a radical rhetoric which, in the case of Castlebrook University in particular, made many promises in terms of students' learning experiences. The willingness on the part of the case-study institutions to present a seemingly radical equal opportunities policy approach in relation to the recruitment of students and curriculum content cannot be entirely divorced from economic motivations.

Staff recruitment and training
While all the case-study universities had made policy statements in this area, there was an equivocism as to the aims of the policies in relation to staff recruitment and training. On the one hand, the documentation in all four case studies made a number of statements as to their commitment to build a representative staff profile in terms of gender, ethnicity and disability. For example, Peoples University claimed that, 'the University aims to increase the recruitment of staff from under-represented groups and ensure that recruitment procedures are free from direct and indirect discriminatory effects ... we aim to recruit at least 3 per cent of staff with disabilities and raise significantly the proportion of black staff by 1995' (*Equal Opportunities Action Plan*, 1990: 8). On the other hand, there was a return, in the policy documentation relating to staff recruitment, to an emphasis on anti-discrimination practices. Ensuring that recruitment procedures are not discriminatory was a theme that ran through all the policy statements in this area, accompanied by recommendations that would enable fairer competition. For example, while Northfield University and Russell College both placed an emphasis on the need to increase staff from minority ethnic groups, they both only cited advertising in minority press publications as a way to do this. Similarly, flexible working hours, childcare and maternity provision were also widely referred to by all the case studies. Training was particularly advocated by three of the case-study universities (Northfield, Peoples and Castlebrook) as one of the primary ways to ensure that recruitment procedures would not be discriminatory. For example, Northfield University stated it was currently pursuing a programme in which at least one member of every selection panel would have undergone training in equal opportunities in terms of legislation and the university's own policies. Russell College echoed this aim and highlighted its 1993 appointment of a staff training and development officer as part of this commitment, and Peoples University declared that a comprehensive staff training programme 'needs to be established and will be in place by 1993' (*Equal Opportunities Action Plan*, 1990: 10). Training, then, was a key theme in the equal opportunities policy statements in relation to staff. For example, Castlebrook University prioritized a comprehensive training and education programme for all staff on equal opportunities legislation and on the university's equal opportunities policies, and noted 'that this programme should be particularly geared to helping staff carry out their duties in a non-discriminatory way' (*Making Equal Opportunities Work*, 1993: 12). The policy makes the significant distinction between staff development on equal opportunities and equal opportunities in staff development. In this latter category, the policy document stated that all managers responsible for training and development of staff must ensure that such training and development opportunities –

sabbaticals, secondment, in-house and external training – are allocated fairly and without discrimination. The policy also recommended that all training and development events for staff should include an equal opportunities dimension.

Within the area of staff employment and development, there is a significant return in the policy documentation to a more liberal interpretation of equal opportunities. Although some rhetorical claims are made as to the case studies wishing to recruit a more representative staff profile, the emphasis is on anti-discrimination practices, on the removal of barriers which might impede the operation of fair competition (e.g. childcare provision, advertising in minority press) and on the training of staff to ensure the implementation of non-discriminatory procedures. There is, then, a degree of contradiction between an institutional willingness to address student issues within a more radical equal opportunities framework, and institutional unwillingness to address staffing and employment issues within the same framework. The case-study universities' policy approaches to staff recruitment can be understood as being located within a liberal equal opportunities framework.

Language guides

Although all of the case-study universities had, to a greater or lesser extent, some form of policy documentation on equal opportunities statements of commitment, harassment policies and equal opportunities in academic affairs, they did not all have language guides. Language guides represent an attempt to address the wider ethos or culture of an organization. Both Peoples University and Northfield University had introduced language guides. Like equal opportunities policy statements and the sexual and racial harassment codes, the language guides were a widely distributed documentary aspect of these universities' equal opportunities programmes, and as with the harassment codes, language guides had proved to be an area of contention. In Northfield University the language guide had been developed through the Equal Opportunities Committee (chaired by the director), and in Peoples University the guide had been written on behalf of the Equal Opportunities Unit (located within the vice-chancellor's office). In other words, both guides had the nominal support of senior management.

Both guides were intended for use in course production, written and audio-visual material and in all written material from memos to publicity statements made in relation to the universities. Both guides clearly stated in their introductions that they also, equally, applied to spoken language. In many ways, the language guides appeared as the most politically ambitious of the equal opportunity policy texts. Not only is there no legislative framework within which to justify their existence, but language guides focus on what is culturally appropriate linguistically within the institution and they centralize the crucial role of language's ability to exclude, stereotype and damage. For example, Northfield University rather sweepingly stated in the opening paragraph of its guide that:

> The University recognises that in the development of equal opportunities, language is not neutral. It is the policy of the University to use the language in a way that conveys this commitment at large and to use the language advocated by national bodies concerned with equal opportunities. The use of appropriate language . . . supports relationships of mutual respect. In addition it contributes to combating all forms of prejudice and eliminating all forms of unfair discrimination.
>
> (*Language and Equal Opportunities Guide*, 1992: 1)

Peoples University made a similar introduction:

> One of the ways in which the University can achieve this aim is through increasing awareness of Equal Opportunities issues in the content and presentation of all its communications. As communicators we have a responsibility both to give a true picture of society and to avoid discriminating against any sections of it . . . Language reflects and enshrines the values and prejudices of the society in which it has evolved, and is a powerful means of perpetuating them.
>
> (*Language and Image Guide*, 1992: 2)

The structure of the guides was also similar, providing a number of categories with recommendations of what words, phrases and terms to use and which to avoid and why. Both guides had categories relating to race, gender, disability and sexuality. However, there was some diversity in terms of additional categories. Peoples University included a category on using plain English and accessible language and Northfield University included a section on the removal of hierarchy in internal and external correspondence, arguing that no individual, academic or status-based titles are necessary or should be used other than 'where it would be detrimental to the standing of the University to omit academic titles'. Although this attempt to flatten out hierarchies is commendable – in an interview conducted with the director of Northfield University, he told me that even senior management did not have reserved places in the university's car park – in the course of the research interesting configurations arose. Not only was the use of academic titles discouraged in internal communications, but the common practice of putting academic status on office doors was similarly discouraged. Yet compliance with this recommendation varied from individual to individual and from department to department. One example of this was in the university's science department, where most of the academics retained the traditional practice of displaying their doctoral status. Yet, significantly, the department's equal opportunities worker, a young black woman who had a PhD, was the only academic who did not have her doctorate title displayed and had not been consulted as to whether she did or did not want her title on her door. In this situation, cosmetic attempts to flatten hierarchies actually served to further marginalize this respondent's position (her brief was to encourage access, especially from the local minority community, to science courses) and minimize her academic status within the department. For black and other minority ethnic academics and for women academics, their status can be particularly important, as these groups are not automatically associated with 'high' academic attainment.

Although the intentions of language guides may be positive, they are very difficult policy documents to introduce within an institution. Not only can they produce contradictory situations, but they can be overly didactic and lead to resentment and ridicule, which in turn can be damaging to the wider equal opportunities programme. Language guides need to be promoted with care within a broader context of equal opportunities. In both Peoples University and Northfield University, there had been widespread hostility to the language guides. Northfield University had received negative accounts of its policy in the local newspaper. At Peoples University, an internal staff newspaper published many letters of condemnation, stating that 'things had gone too far' or that the guides represented the 'thought police' and an 'attack on academic freedom of expression' (*Staff Newsletter*, November 1992). Although such attacks on the language guides may be predictable in their nature, this does not detract from their potential to inflict damage on equal opportunities policies. The frequency with which language guides were cited (within my interviews) as examples of 'lunacy' and 'political correctness' demonstrated this.

Other equal opportunities documentation

The equal opportunity policy statements, the sexual and racial harassment codes of practice, the language guides and the equal opportunities in academic affairs documents all represented the basis of the policy literature in the case studies. The remaining equal opportunities documentation tended to relate to the practice of the equal opportunities structures that were in place in the individual institutions. This documentation usually took the form of the annual reports of the Equal Opportunities Committees from the four universities, and from the specialized race, gender and equal opportunities units which existed in Northfield University and Peoples University.

Usually, the annual reports of the Equal Opportunities Committees took a fairly upbeat, 'we're getting there' tone. For example, Peoples University's *Equal Opportunities Report* (1992: 9–10) concludes:

> Resource constraints have impeded some progress and progress has not always been easy, but, nevertheless, there are solid achievements . . . openness and equality are the cornerstone of the University and the [University] aims to ensure that these principles are put into practice.

The annual reports all had a tendency to draw on monitoring data to cite 'improvements' – that is, increases in the numbers of students from minority ethnic groups or increases in women students in traditionally male disciplines. The reports also shared a tendency to outline the main areas to which the Equal Opportunities Committees and related structures had addressed themselves during the year. For example, Castlebrook's *Annual Report of the Equal Opportunities Committee* (1992–93) simply listed its activities for that year – the re-writing of its equality policies, the establishment of equal opportunities training programmes for staff sitting on selection panels, ethnic monitoring surveys for students – and confirmed that it liaised closely with the Disability Committee.

Significantly, none of the annual reports attempted a serious evaluation of the effectiveness of the institutions' equality policies in an in-depth way. Overwhelmingly, the annual reports were descriptive. They demonstrated little tendency towards being self-critical, reflexive or analytical. The effectiveness or ineffectiveness of an equal opportunities policy was measured in monitoring terms alone.

Of the four universities, only Northfield had attempted, in the late 1980s, to make a more qualitative and evaluatory inquiry into women's equality within the university. Perhaps most importantly, this inquiry was conducted by an external researcher which led to the publication of a detailed report. This report was generally critical of the university's gender equality initiatives and made a number of policy and structural recommendations to amend this position, including the establishment of a Women's Unit. Although at the time of my research the university had implemented a number of these recommendations – most notably the Women's Unit and the three advisory sub-committees – it had by no means implemented all of the report's recommendations and no follow-up report was planned by the university. However, that Northfield University had commissioned an independent, external review of its gender equality policies indicated a broader commitment on the part of the institution to a more in-depth and reflexive approach to the issues. The timing of the report is significant – the research was commissioned in the late 1980s when equal opportunities had a much higher profile in many organizations' activities and agendas (Lansley, 1989; Cockburn, 1992).

Critical readings of equal opportunities documentation

Silences

The variations in the case-study universities' equal opportunities documentation can be understood as reflecting a wider picture of equal opportunities within different institutions. The glossily packaged and senior management endorsed equal opportunities documents of Castlebrook University indicated the support and dominance of senior management in the university's equality-making processes. The more extensive equal opportunities

documentation of both Peoples University and Northfield University indicated an institutional history of engagement with equal opportunities issues.
Conversely, the limited and scattered documentation of Russell College
implied that equal opportunities occupied a low status and peripheral
position within the institution. However, despite these variations, there was
a degree of standardization in terms of the areas each case-study university
had targeted for equal opportunities policy generation: formal statements
of commitment, harassment policies and academic affairs. The policy documents all shared a tendency to approach equal opportunities in a highly
mechanical and technicist way with an emphasis on such issues as monitoring, training, non-discriminatory practice and representation.

The documentation in all the case studies revealed ambiguous and often
converged rhetoric in terms of the objectives of equal opportunities policies
– at certain points representation was the key aim of the policy and at other
times non-discrimination was the policy goal. There were also important
silences which all the documents shared. The notions of power, social justice,
oppression and domination were very rarely, and certainly never overtly,
discussed in the equal opportunities policy texts. Similarly, the term 'anti-
racism' was conspicuously absent from all the policy statements. The practice documentation did not attempt to use a reflexive or self-critical approach
in assessing the effectiveness of the equality policies, nor did it acknowledge the difficulties of implementing policies, in the everyday world of
institutions. In reading this presentational data, what becomes increasingly
important is what policy documents do not say rather than what they do say
or claim. In many ways, the gaps and silences of the universities' equal
opportunities policy texts became one of their most significant features.

Condensation symbols

Besides silence one of the dominant features of the universities' equal opportunities documentation, was the extensive and shared use of 'condensation symbols' (Edelman, 1964), 'slogan systems' (Apple, 1977) or 'essentially
contested concepts' (Gallie, 1956). Condensation symbols, slogan systems
and essentially contested concepts refer to terms or phrases that contain a
particular emotional impact and positive associations while at the same time
retain an elasticity which means that they understood in a variety of competing ways. Most obvious is the term 'equal opportunities' itself, but such
terms as 'equality', 'justice', 'multiculturalism' and 'access' also constitute
condensation symbols. The discourses associated with these phrases often
conceal conflicting ideologies and a diversity of interests for those involved
in policy-making and implementation processes. As Vincent (1993: 231) has
noted:

> The exact meaning of condensation symbols is rarely clearly defined.
> Indeed they are often kept vague to attract as much support as possible.

Over time, the words and phrases gain assumed meanings which are rarely critically scrutinised. This means that their usage can obscure more than they can illuminate.

While it is not clear whether policy-makers use condensation symbols consciously (Troyna and Williams, 1986) or unconsciously (Edelman, 1977), what is clear is that condensation symbols create ambiguities within policy texts and the frequent use of highly familiar phrases results in standardized policy guidelines that are unreflexive and mechanical. Wendy Ball (1994) argues that another aspect of this standardization can mean that the policy process can become an end in itself. For example, the primary concern begins to be 'getting the wording right' (1994: 5). Within this context, one of my central concerns in my interviews was to attempt to probe and 'unpack' the term 'equal opportunities'. While it worked as a condensation symbol in the policy statements, what did the term actually mean to those who generated and wrote the policy documents? In keeping with the nature of condensation symbols, respondents from both the senior management group and from those formally involved with equal opportunities struggled with this question. The following examples from senior management respondents illustrate the difficulty of definition:

SN: What is your own understanding or definition of equal opportunities?

Director (Northfield University): It means for me what it says in our statement, that we are seeking to eradicate unfair discrimination. Higher education is a highly discriminating environment. For example, students get different marks for essays every day of the week. What is important is that the differences reflect the application of clearly known criteria applied in a fair way. That has got to be a process that takes place independent of people's race, people's gender, people's age, religion, etc. So we work and live in a very discriminating environment, but that's all right for me, as long as it is on fair principles that are understood. What we are seeking to do here is eradicate unfair discrimination and I think that is what equal opportunities is about for me.

Pro-vice-chancellor, Programme Development, (Peoples University): I'm not sure I have a snap definition for you. I suppose it's to do with making sure there are no inherent discriminations going on in things like recruitment. As far as the curriculum is concerned, it's to do with making sure the material is not off-putting to particular groups, that it's not just men and women, it's ethnicity and disability as well. So I suppose it's about making sure that doors are not shut that could be open and making sure that prejudices and assumptions don't come into play. But the matching of a person to a person specification is what matters.

University secretary (Northfield University): I haven't got a very strong theoretical definition. I think what drives me on equal opportunities is the fairness issue, a sort of equal treatment type of issue, more of a humane issue is what I'm saying, rather than a legally based one. I have a strong sense of fair play. I can't stand it when people don't play fair or don't treat people fair and that's not really a gender or race issue, that's a human type of issue.

What becomes apparent in these responses is an adherence to liberal understanding of equal opportunities which centre on the notions of fairness and non-discrimination. It was equally significant that the replies to the same question, when asked of those respondents who were formally responsible for the case-study universities' equal opportunities policies, tended also to be couched in very similar terms as those of senior management:

Equal Opportunities Director (Peoples University): I think I take it from a fairly pragmatic viewpoint. There has been a lot of work done on the principles of equity and equal treatment and justice in the concept of equality, and although I'm interested in that debate I'm more interested in trying to ensure that, as an institution, the university offers a really fair deal to students and staff regardless of all the usual things – gender, race, ethnic origin and disability.

Personnel officer with responsibility for equal opportunities in staffing (Russell College): Good grief! I suppose it's as far as possible to widen the choice for . . . talking in recruitment, selection, promotion and training terms, access to as many people as possible in any level of the organization.

Chair of the Race Advisory Group (Northfield University): Well I haven't thought about it, although I probably speak a lot and hopefully do a lot about it.

Equal opportunities convenor for education department (Russell College): I see it as . . . well, that people should be given opportunities based on their abilities . . . but not just based on their belonging to certain categories.

Women's unit co-ordinator (Northfield University): My understanding? That's difficult. I suppose for me it's about ensuring that certain groups aren't discriminated against and that there is a much fairer representation of those people . . . women, ethnic minorities . . . people with disabilities . . . groups who have been traditionally excluded.

What is significant here is that defining the concept of equal opportunities was problematic for those respondents who had a direct role in implementing equal opportunities in their universities.

It was the third target group – respondents who were indirectly/informally involved in equal opportunities issues – from whom there was the widest critical assessment of the concept of equal opportunities. Again this is significant, because this group was only marginally, if at all, involved in the equality policy-making processes and this group was made up almost entirely of academics whose professional and political interests were in researching and writing in related areas. For example:

Senior lecturer, social science faculty (Northfield University): I'm pretty cynical about equal opportunities really. I'm interested in the politics of equal opportunities, the way in which equal opportunities is the acceptable face of equality, access and so on. Equal opportunities in this institution, and probably nationally, has very little to say. When I hear the phrase 'equal opportunities', even though I'm using it myself all the time, I think it is about a very limited agenda for making minor adjustments within the *status quo* for making things fairer, basically just to expand slightly the band of people who are getting on.

Senior lecturer, education faculty (Northfield University): My view of equal opportunities is simply not about the removal of barriers for people's full participation. It must be about the positive intervention in most processes, most educational processes, rather than passively responding to situations as they arise. It is about the positive acknowledgement of what people bring to the institution and making sure that gets appropriately rewarded. Yes, you do have to try and get rid of barriers, but it is much more than that.

Research fellow, policy studies unit (Russell College): I would adopt a far more critical approach to equal opportunities than anything that the university does. I see equal opportunities as arising from a liberal philosophy of equality, equal rights, which doesn't necessarily challenge a power structure in terms of class or patriarchy or racism or heteropatriarchy. I think when we look at equal opportunities developing within an institution, equal opportunities practices, we are looking very much at a liberal philosophy rather than something that is ultimately challenging to the system.

So while critical voices did exist, these were minority voices and they came from people who tended to be on the peripheries of equal opportunities policy-making and implementation processes within the case studies.

While the term 'anti-racism' was not a common feature within the policy text, I did ask all respondents in my interviews what they took anti-racism to mean and whether they saw it as separate or inclusive to the equal opportunities rubric. Not surprisingly, this too was perceived as a 'difficult' question. Overwhelmingly, anti-racism was defined as meaning 'not discriminating against black people'. While Gilroy (1990: 207) has warned that 'we should be wary of collapsing anti-racism, let alone black emancipation into equal opportunities', the majority of respondents located anti-racism within the equal opportunities rubric and there was a tendency to reduce anti-racism into the (more comfortable) notion of racial equality:

Chair of Race Advisory Committee (Northfield University): Anti-racism is about racial equality, about not discriminating on the basis of skin colour ... about not making negative judgements about things like different cultures.

Clearly, 'anti-racism' as a condensation symbol has severe limitations and its absence from the policy texts can in part be understood within this context. Unlike 'equal opportunities', 'anti-racism' lacks the necessary degree of vagueness or elasticity and its connotations are not unequivocally positive – that is, its usage does not provoke the ideas of harmony, consensus or joint endeavour. There was some evidence in the interviews that the high-profile anti-anti-racist attacks from the Right and the media during the 1980s had had some impact on higher education – anti-racism was negatively associated with political municipal campaigns – and this fed into an institutional avoidance of policies that could be specifically labelled as anti-racist:

> *Head of human resources (Castlebrook University)*: I'm not in favour of separating out policies for black students and staff. I'm very critical of organizations that have done that in the past . . . like ILEA and some of the other London boroughs . . . all equal opportunities aspects are as important as the others.

The lack of references to anti-racism in the policy texts and its collapse into equal opportunities in the interviews is a reflection of the problematic status of anti-racism within higher education's equality discourses.

Marketing and public relations

Wendy Ball (1994: 6) notes that 'in the language of equal opportunities, rhetoric plays a crucial role in presenting a particular image of an institution'. While key phrases – condensation symbols – may have a plethora of contested meanings outside of policy rhetoric, this does not detract from the ability of that rhetoric to be a meaningful tool in creating (and presenting) positive or desired images of institutions: 'It is conceivable that individual actors, groups or establishments will utilise a rhetoric without any ideological conviction as regards its validity, but with a recognition of its pragmatic efficacy' (Ball, 1979: 202–203). When an institution declares itself committed to equal opportunities a number of motivations can be involved in this (Morgan and Knights, 1991; Cockburn, 1992; Heward and Taylor, 1993; Ball, 1994; Farish *et al.*, 1995). There were indications in the two 'new' case-study universities that economic considerations had played a role in these institutions' willingness to present a public equal opportunities face, especially in terms of student recruitment. Prior to gaining university status, both Northfield and Castlebrook Universities had pursued expansionist strategies, an element of which included appealing to 'non-traditional' students. Since gaining university status, both Northfield and Castlebrook had been caught between the economic need to expand and the cultural concern to increase academic prestige. The idea that these two processes were detrimental to each other was a recurring theme that emerged in interviews with senior management respondents at both 'new' universities. For example, when interviewing the pro-vice-chancellor at Castlebrook University he continually expressed his concern that the university was viewed by the 'old' higher education establishment as a 'mickey mouse university' because of its close associations with the local (inner-city) community and non-traditional students:

> *SN*: Is that [the mickey mouse label] a particular worry for the university then?

> *PVC*: It is and it isn't . . . we're very proud here of our access routes and that we can provide a second chance for people to have a higher education . . . we'd never want to break our links with the local community . . . but we also want to appeal to those students with a more traditional profile, a three 'A' level profile, as well.

This same theme also emerged, although from a different perspective, in an interview with a senior lecturer in the university's social science faculty:

> When these places [new universities] were trying to expand they made wonderful, high sounding noises about equal opportunities, but as soon as they feel they have to compete and they're called universities and they want to look good, then they'll throw it all out of the window.

Policy rhetoric also raises expectations on the part of certain groups. When an institution appears to have a strong commitment to equal opportunities, there is also the danger that there will be a very real shortfall between the expectations of those groups which such an equal opportunities 'identity' specifically attracts and their actual experiences of the institution. This gap was commented on by a number of respondents as the following excerpts from interview transcripts demonstrate:

> *SN*: Do you think that there is a public relations aspect to equal opportunities at the university?

> *Professor, education faculty (Castlebrook University)*: the university has marketed itself very much as being committed to equal opportunities and this raises expectations. There is a lot of anger and bitterness among black students . . . not just because they experience racism here but because their expectations haven't been met, and that in a way is even more damaging . . . it's a deception . . . black students feel they have been deceived.

There were direct echoes of this in response to the same question when asked of a senior lecturer in the social science faculty in Northfield University:

> There is a dilemma with equal opportunities rhetoric . . . the need to show people that you're trying and then those groups who have traditionally had a bad deal in higher education may think that perhaps this place [the university] will give me a better deal . . . there is a need to

do that if you don't want those people to be put off instantly, but the balance between doing that and giving misleading or false impressions seems to me to be a tricky one. I think we've gone too far. I think public relations work now dominates and there is a lack of honesty about what we are able to achieve and what we're not able to achieve.

An interesting and rather bizarre flip side to the public relations and/or economic benefits of equal opportunities policies surfaced in Russell College, where the main 'social drama' in relation to equal opportunities while I was doing the fieldwork was an attempt to establish a new, updated equal opportunities statement for the institution. The central area of contention voiced by some members of the Equal Opportunities Committee, including the chair (a senior member of the directorate), was the inclusion of sexuality and sexual orientation in the categories which the university formally states it would not discriminate on. The micro-politics of this situation highlight broader issues about the place of equal opportunities discourses and policies within higher education. For example, in my interview with the Director of Russell College, I asked why the inclusion of sexual orientation was so problematic:

I think there is unease about sexual orientation. When you move from the Equal Opportunities Committee into the public arena and public statements there is a major problem in what you say in things like the prospectus . . . in a Muslim country there is complete and total hostile reaction. The kind of issues that may disturb us in this country are perceived as very Eurocentric ones by people on the Indian sub-continent who say 'we don't know what you are talking about and what kind of place is this which is fussing away with these issues?' They are uncomfortable with the notion of entering a society where this is so . . . nobody is saying it shouldn't exist . . . but where it is so thrown at them, something to which they don't subscribe to at all. They are worried to come and study where there are things about sexual orientation going on . . . this is a *nightmare* for some of them. There are so many other things that they want from the university and we are anxious not to say well don't come (emphasis added).

This response is significant for a number of reasons. First, it highlights deep unease about certain aspects of the equal opportunities discourse (i.e. sexuality) and the validity of this within equality policy statements (see Chapter 6). Second, it illustrates the notion and fear that equal opportunities statements can actually harm an institution (especially economically). It is significant that it is overseas students, who represent a lucrative source of income, who are being referred to here. Third, the entire rationale of this respondent's position rests on new racist discourses using 'illiberal' and 'pre-modern' Muslim/other and liberal modern 'western' stereotypes (see Gillborn, 1995).

Conclusion

This chapter has concentrated on the presentational data – the equal opportunities policy documents – readily made available to me by all four case-study universities. This documentation varied between the institutions both in visual terms and in terms of quantity. I have argued that such variations reflect the differing institutional contexts in which the equal opportunities policies were generated. However, despite such variations, there was a degree of standardization in the equal opportunities documentation of all the case studies. There were certain common areas which the policy documents tended to cover: harassment, student recruitment, teaching/curriculum content and staff recruitment. The policy documents shared a converged liberal/radical equal opportunities rhetoric and a tendency to construct equality policy approaches through a mechanical and technicist framework. The extensive use of condensation symbols/slogan systems in the language of the policy documents disguises the contested meanings of the key concepts on which the documents rest. Accompanying the use of condensation symbols were shared silences in the documentation, particularly in relation to the more contentious political dimensions of equal opportunities and the concept/strategy of anti-racism. As Wendy Ball (1994: 3) argues 'institutions' policy texts serve a variety of purposes and cannot be taken at face value'. An institution's willingness to demonstrate a commitment to equal opportunities can become divorced from issues of social justice and become tangled up with public relations, marketing concerns and the projection of a desired image. However, the relationship between an institution's desired image and its equal opportunities commitment can also become highly ambiguous, as is evident in the 'mickey mouse' concerns of Castlebrook University's senior management or Russell College's anxieties over the inclusion of a sexuality dimension in its equal opportunities statement. In probing the equal opportunities policy texts, what became increasingly apparent was the messy, contested and fractured everyday world of the case studies. It is this world that the following chapter explores.

5

Equality Policies in the Everyday World of Universities

Introduction

While the equal opportunities policy texts did often demonstrate an amalgamation between liberal and radical interpretations the texts also represent a sanitized and rationalized version of an institution's equal opportunities intentions. In other words, while different and competing understandings of the concept of equal opportunities may be disguised in policy declarations and statements, the actual implementation of those policies, of moving from policy to practice, is a process which presents sites in which those differences often acrimoniously emerge and thereby limit the successful working of equality policies.

As Young (1989: 96) argues, 'where a policy is founded upon ambiguity, any apparent consensus is likely to be fragile and incapable of withstanding the stresses and conflicts of implementation'. In the everyday world of organizations, equal opportunities – as a discourse and as policy – becomes a terrain which is characterized by struggle and contention. For example, in their research into local politics and race in Liverpool and Wolverhampton, Ben-Tovim et al. (1986) comment on the 'prevalent tendency within local government to push anti-racist forces away from the centre towards the periphery of local politics and policy provision' and they argue that 'local struggles against racism have become struggles against marginalization' (p. 100).

Similarly Ouseley (1984, 1990) has highlighted how equality units, committees, advisers – usually on low grades and with overall low status – have simply been 'grafted' onto broader local government structures which may be reluctant to acknowledge discriminatory or exclusive practices and are often resistant to attempts to try to change such practices. Ouseley (1984: 144) suggests that this has made specialist (equality) structures 'easy targets for bureaucracies to isolate, thus reducing further their potential and scope for getting close enough to power structures to challenge them'. Alongside the issue of marginalization commentators like Anthias and Yuval-Davis (1992) have examined the complexities in terms of whom equal opportunities policies should be working for and the resultant fragmented and competitive hierarchy that can develop from this.

For example, they recount a bitter dispute between Greater London Council's Race Unit and its Women's Unit as to which had prior claim to a newly appointed black woman worker (1992: 172). Anthias and Yuval-Davis argue that the anti-discriminatory orientations of equal opportunities thinking and policy making divorces the equal opportunities rubric from issues of 'structural disadvantage': 'there is an assumption within equal opportunities strategies that it is discriminatory practices which produce disadvantage and discriminatory practices alone' (1992: 174).

Ambiguity as to what equal opportunities means and what the aims of equality policies should be; the separation of equal opportunities from a broader social justice framework; marginalization, fragmentation and the development of competitive hierarchies are all macro-political processes which manifest themselves in the micro-politics of organizational settings (Ball, 1987; Blase, 1991; Weiner, 1992; Ball, 1994). Within this context this chapter examines the way in which equal opportunities policies in the case study universities were contested and surrounded by tensions and contradictions. Drawing on the glimpses into the messy everyday world of the four higher education institutions that the research afforded, the chapter considers the *ownership* of equal opportunities policies, the *marginalization* of both equality structures and equality issues and the development of a fragmented *hierarchy* within equal opportunities discourses.

Ownership of equal opportunities policies

In all four case-study universities, equal opportunities discourses and policy-making were heavily influenced by senior management. In other words, equal opportunities was constructed according to a top-down model. This created the ironic situation of equality issues being firmly located within the remit of the highest level of the institutions' hierarchy – senior management. The irony of this situation was further compounded by the masculinity of management – that is, managing is an activity concerned with 'male' qualities of functionality, rationality, leadership and instrumentalism (Burton, 1993). In the case-study universities, the senior management teams were overwhelmingly male (I interviewed only three women in senior management teams) and all were white. This masculinity was often reflected in the ways in which equality policies were often pushed forward through the institution in a manner which can be against the spirit or ethos of equal opportunities more generally (i.e. in a non-democratic, non-consultative way):

> Directives just arrive from above here . . . I received one today which informs us that we must no longer say 'ethnic minorities', we must now say 'minority ethnics', it's ridiculous . . . I don't understand why we now have to say this instead of that. We're just told from above.
>
> (Lecturer, science department)

The top-down equal opportunities model was particularly pronounced in Northfield and Castlebrook Universities. In Northfield University, the director who had been in post prior to my research was commonly identified as being the driving force for introducing the university's first and entire equal opportunities programme. The director who had succeeded him, although not perceived as being quite so personally committed to equality issues, had adopted a similar position and identified himself as the vanguard of the policy programme. For example, *Women's Unit Handbook* contained a section which explained the existence of the Equal Opportunities Committee and stated that anybody could put an item for discussion on the committee's agenda by contacting the Director (*Women's Unit Handbook*, 1993: 3). I explored this further in my interview with the university's director:

SN: What do you see as the role of the senior management team in relation to equal opportunities in the university?

Director: We have an Equal Opportunities Committee which I chair and this is technically a committee that is *advisory to me* and it is the vehicle by which our major policy initiatives and procedures are discussed, put forward and taken, *via myself*, to the appropriate bodies which might be the management team, the University Board and the Academic Board and so I see myself as having responsibility for taking those issues forward. The formality side involves disciplinary procedures, for example our sexual harassment policy and procedure is one in which if a person makes a complaint, then it has to be investigated according to procedure but that procedure *ends with a report to me and me deciding* whether then to invoke disciplinary procedures. The less formal side is the debating of the policies and putting forward new ideas, encouraging new thoughts about these things. Initiatives do come from all over the university but it is *my task* to make sure that they get debated at places like the Equal Opportunities Committee (emphasis added).

The perception of the role of senior management displayed here clearly involves control and veto. Similarly, the Director of Russell College stated:

Senior management have got to set the standards and be fairly tough about maintaining those standards. I chair the Equal Opportunities Committee because it's important that the committee has some weight and status ... senior management have to be seen to be leading the way in these issues.

The notion that senior management's role was to 'lead from the top' and the argument that senior management's presence as chairs on Equal Opportunity Committees gave those committees 'weight and status' were commonly expressed in all my interviews with senior management figures. The top-down model had severely affected both the actual ownership of equality policies and, perhaps even more significantly, the *perception* of ownership of the policies. This narrow ownership of the equal opportunities policies

occurred despite the existence of (often extensive) equal opportunity structures within the universities (see Chapter 2 for a list of these structures).

In Castlebrook University, equal opportunities issues were dominated by
a very small, six-member Equal Opportunities Committee, which was made
up almost entirely of senior management team members with only one
place given to a member of the university's teaching staff. This committee
had only recently been formed, replacing a large and elected committee.
Although there had been some resentment by equal opportunities 'activists' in the university to this development, opposition had never been suf-
ficiently organized to seriously challenge this reorganization. When I asked
the only staff representative on the committee about the democratic processes of the committee, she told me: 'There are no democratic concerns
on that committee . . . it's just managerialism . . . and the whole university is
dominated by managerialism'.

The committee had set itself the task of re-writing the equal opportunities policies for the institution and the document, glossily packaged, was
launched on the university by simply distributing it to every staff member
and incorporating it into the student handbook. The nature of the Equal
Opportunities Committee and the total absence of any consultative process
in the re-development of the policy documents meant that there was a very
low level of ownership of the equal opportunities policies at Castlebrook.
Unlike Northfield University, at Castlebrook University this lack of ownership was primarily expressed, not in terms of hostility to the policies themselves, but through a lack of awareness of (and desire to know) what the
policies actually even were. A number of respondents in this case study told
me how they had just found the policy documents in their pigeon holes and
had not yet read them. These were often respondents who saw themselves
as having a specific interest and/or commitment to equality issues:

> Well I just found it in my tray actually. It looks very smart and expens-
> ive but I haven't got around to looking at it yet. I support equal
> opportunities and think it's really important but how much this has
> been discussed . . . I don't know.
>
>   (Lecturer, social science faculty)

The very narrow ownership of equal opportunities policies at Castlebrook
was underlined by the absence of any additional equal opportunities
structures.

In Peoples University, the focus of equal opportunities activity was the
Equal Opportunities Unit. However, the structural location of this unit,
within the vice-chancellor's office, meant that inevitably the unit was closely
associated with the university's senior management team. As at Castlebrook
University, the Equal Opportunities Committee at Peoples University was a
small committee dominated by senior management figures. Each faculty at
Peoples University has an equal opportunities convenor. As one convenor
explained:

While our policies do come through the Equal Opportunities Unit at the same time they're coming through the vice-chancellor's office, because that's where the unit has been placed . . . so equal opportunities comes from the hierarchy and the management, but usually they just pass things back out to the committees and come out with the right rhetoric.

I am not arguing against the need for senior management to adopt a high-profile commitment to equal opportunities within the institutions. The support of powerful people does give equal opportunities policies status. The lack of such commitment can mean that there is very little activity pushing through equality policy development. This tended to be the case in Russell College where, despite the director's assertion that senior management should lead from the top, there was very little support or initiation from that level. However, an over-emphasis on the top-down models can serve both to silence other voices or points of activity/pressure and remove ownership of policies from the main body of the institution, resulting at best in a lack of interest, knowledge and involvement and at worst in feelings of alienation, resentment and hostility.

Equality policies which lack a broad base of ownership are immediately restricted and limited in terms of effectiveness. In many ways, it is difficult not to give a more 'sinister' reading of senior management's interest in developing and implementing equal opportunities policies. In other words, can the willingness of senior management to lend support to equality policies be seen simply as an altruistic desire to give those policies and issues status, or is it that, as the most powerful group within institutions, senior management can set, control and police the equality agenda? From the research it would appear that in all four case studies, both these functions were fulfilled by the position taken by the institutions' hierarchies. In other words, senior management's ownership of, and proximity to, equality initiatives can be both enabling and disabling.

Marginalization

Marginalization of equality structures

As I noted earlier, a number of commentators (Solomos, 1983; Ouseley, 1984; Ben-Tovim *et al.*, 1986; Anthias and Yuval-Davis, 1992) have argued that equality initiatives and the structures put in place to implement them have a particular vulnerability to being pushed to the very edges of an organization's activities and priorities. There was evidence of the marginalization of equal opportunities structures in all of the case-study universities. However, the processes of marginalization were not as extensive at Castlebrook as the university had such limited equality structures. This absence of structures can be understood as part of a broader marginalization of equal opportunities concerns within the institution. At one level the occurrence of marginalization may seem at odds with senior management support for/ownership of equal opportunities. However, at another level, the marginalization of equality structures concurs with the anti-democratic style of equality policy-making in the case study universities and the argument made above that the 'heavy' senior management of equal opportunities reflected a strategy of control and constraint rather than genuine concerns with issues of social justice.

Marginalization tended to occur with those equality structures additional to each case-study university's central equal opportunities committees (i.e. those structures in which senior management figures were not directly involved). For example, in Russell College, a system in which all academic and non-academic departments appointed a staff member as an equal opportunities consultant had been in place since 1986. These consultants met as a group three times a year and fed issues via the equal opportunities officer to the Equal Opportunities Committee.

The terms of reference for the consultants were that they would be in place for three years and that they should volunteer or be appointed by the heads of the departments. Their main tasks and responsibilities were to provide a focus for all matters relating to equality issues in their departments through such strategies as advising and informing colleagues about equal opportunities policies, collecting resource material and generally raising awareness regarding equality issues. The consultants were to act as the first point of contact for staff and students in the department to raise matters of concern, including complaints, relating to equality issues. The consultants were also expected to undertake training to increase their knowledge and understanding of equal opportunities issues to develop the skills necessary to deal with them in the workplace (*Terms of Reference for Equal Opportunities Consultants*, 1990).

In practice, however, the consultants in place at the time of the research had either been there for a number of years, well beyond the three-year stipulation, or had only just taken on the role, which was often pushed on the most recent staff to join the department. The consultant's role was a difficult one to fill, because there was a general reluctance to take it on. The majority of the consultants did not have any senior status within the departments and had usually been coerced into accepting it by a head of department or had taken it because 'nobody else wanted to do it'. Overwhelmingly, the consultants were women. There was a very low level of activity among the consultants and only a small minority – well under half – attended the three yearly meetings. Such was the ineffectiveness of the consultant system that at the time of my research, the whole system was under review. In interviews with the consultants, what became apparent was both the respondents' openly admitted lack of understanding about what they were actually supposed to do – none of them had actually received any training – and their conception of equal opportunities as being about specific 'problems' or 'complaints'. In other words, the consultants felt uncertain of what they should be doing if they had no complaints to deal with. In effect, then, the consultants' system was one which was inactive and characterized by apathy – 'if a problem related to equal opportunities comes up, then I do my best to sort it out but otherwise . . .' (Consultant, history department) – and uncertainty:

> I'm a bit ashamed to say I haven't really been involved in anything. I've always gone to the consultants' meetings once a term but I'm not actually sure about my role. I've just taken it on. I was asked to . . . sometimes I think that was because I'm one of the few women in the department. I would like to be more pro-active and I am sympathetic to equal opportunities, but I'm not an expert or anything.
> (Consultant, education department)

Another, similarly marginalized figure at Russell College was the equal opportunities officer. This officer, although committed, had no senior status within the university and had been allocated a three and half hours per week time period to work on equality-related issues. Her very commitment was seen as politically motivated. She felt that she had been very isolated (and labelled) within the university:

> I think I'm seen as a trouble-maker or even as an extremist, as someone who's always going on about the same old things and I am always going on about the same old things but that's because I've got to, because it's such a struggle and when it's like that it does make it seem lonely. There are a few committed people here and we try to support each other, but it is difficult to really get anywhere when there is so little time or money or priority put on the issues.

I found further examples of the overt marginalization of equal opportunities structures in Northfield University. While Russell College and Peoples University had both adopted an integrationist approach to its equal opportunities structures, for example the establishment of an equal opportunities officer (Russell College) and the creation of an Equal Opportunities Unit (Peoples University), Northfield had taken a more separatist approach creating a Racial Equality Centre and a Women's Unit. In 1986, the university had initially used Section 11 money to fund a Race Equality Unit. This unit was made up of eight full-time workers. The remit of the unit (and its workers) had been to conduct race-related advisory work with university departments in relation to research, student liaison, access to higher education and curriculum and staff development. From its establishment, the Race Equality Unit appeared to have been controversial within the university, viewed with suspicion and hostility. As a senior lecturer in the social science department who had been involved with the unit explained to me:

> I don't think people were happy with the Race Equality Unit . . . there were tensions definitely. Staff would talk of it [the unit] in disparaging

ways . . . race spies and that sort of thing. It didn't really have that much power but I think that there was a feeling that it did have power, that it was checking people and that it was just trying to bring black students in.

After moving away from local authority control and with the ending of Section 11 funding, Northfield University completely restructured the Race Equality Unit. In 1991, the unit became the Race Equality Centre and, significantly, this centre became located within the university's Access Unit. The Racial Equality Centre had been devolved by placing five workers in individual academic faculties, leaving just two workers, a coordinator and an administrative worker, in the centre itself. Since restructuring, the remit of the Racial Equality Centre has centred solely around issues of access, outreach work with the local black community and support for black and other minority ethnic students. Through its collection of 'race-related' books, periodicals, journals, press cuttings and videotapes, the centre also acted as a resource base for 'race-related matters'. In other words, the role of the Racial Equality Centre focused largely on the traditional idea of meeting the 'special needs' of black and ethnic minority students. The centre had no involvement with staff recruitment or staff development.

The former Race Equality Unit workers, now known as equal opportunities workers and re-located in individual faculties across the university, were given a brief to work not just with race issues but equality issues more broadly. As with the Racial Equality Centre, staff recruitment and development did not form part of the equal opportunities workers' activities. Despite the restructuring of Northfield's racial equality initiatives, the workers involved in implementing these initiatives were still widely referred to/*stigmatized* as 'Section 11 workers' within the university. The two workers in the Racial Equality Centre and all the equal opportunities workers in the individual faculties were, at the time of the research, black. The ethnic composition of the equal opportunities workers buttressed the commonsense assumption within the university (and more generally) which equates blackness with expertise in 'race-related matters'. Both the stigmatization and expertise themes arose in my discussions with two of the equal opportunities workers. Both respondents explained how they felt that they had only been employed because they were black and because they had doctorates. They felt that because they were black, the university had simply presumed they would 'know what to do' in the post, even though they had limited experience of working in areas of encouraging access:

I'd just finished doing two years post-doctoral research work at an old university. I suppose I just didn't really realize what the job would be here. One of the first things I had to do here was to go to and talk to a local group of Asian women about why they should think about using the university and going into higher education. I didn't have a clue really.

I don't think I've been made so consistently aware that I'm black as since I've been working here. The faculty's all right but you're on your own . . . you're known as the Section 11 worker . . . you're seen as the one who's trying to get more black students in.

The feelings of marginalization and stigmatization were common to all the equal opportunities workers. The originally claimed intention of devolving these workers into individual faculties as a way of integrating them more fully into the university, rather than being clustered in one unit, had in many ways served to equally isolate their position.[1]

Where there was no direct senior management presence, there was evidence of the marginalization of equal opportunities structures and the people who worked within them. The system of designating a particular staff member to take up responsibility for equal opportunities issues in their department/faculty adopted by both Russell College and Peoples University was characterized either by an unwillingness to take up such a responsibility or by the long-term holding of such a post past the policy stipulated time limit. Both of these situations reflect the low status with which equality work was viewed. That those people who were designated equal opportunities responsibilities were often women is significant. Similarly significant was the low level of activity of these staff members and their often expressed uncertainty as to what they should actually be doing in terms of equal opportunities work. Time was also a factor, as staff members with responsibility for equal opportunities issues had to either carry out these in addition to their everyday teaching and research work or were allocated only a minimum number of hours. Marginalization of equal opportunities structures could occur, then, through the generally low prestige of equal opportunities work, the lack of time available to devote to equality-related work and the uncertainty as to what was required. In Northfield University, marginalization processes had their roots in the historical context of the institution – the hostility and suspicion demonstrated towards the Section 11 funded racial equality initiatives. While these initiatives had been reformed and restructured, the stigmatization and suspicion remained and thus continued to isolate those people who were attempting to implement the initiatives.

Marginalization of equality questions

Alongside the marginalization of equal opportunities structures, there was also evidence of the marginalization of equal opportunities issues into certain designated, technicist areas such as access, monitoring, training and 'fair' interviewing. On the one hand, this may be a result of the approaches of the case-study universities' equal opportunities policy documents, but on the other the approach of the documents may be a result of the ways in which equal opportunities issues were initially conceived. Whichever came first, there was an overwhelming tendency to marginalize and/or reduce equality questions into particular categories. For example, in all four case-study universities, questions of racial equality were often collapsed into questions of 'access' and 'special needs'.

Peoples University had written three reports on issues of access in relation to black and minority ethnic students since the late 1980s, but had not produced any reports on black and minority ethnic students' experiences once inside the university (see Bird, 1996). There are damaging consequences to this process of marginalization. Within higher education, debates about 'access' have become part of deracialized discourse, seemingly race-neutral but at the same time carrying racial connotations: 'I really do think that most staff here think that all access students are black and that all black students are access students' (Equal opportunities worker, Northfield University). As notions of racial equality had a tendency to be reduced to 'access' and 'special needs' categories (I discuss this further in the next section), there was evidence of similar reductionist processes being applied within the wider equal opportunities discourse. This occurred mainly in terms of reducing questions of equality and policy implementation into monitoring and personnel procedures. In other words, it was not simply individuals or structures that were marginalized, but broader questions regarding inequality were also being marginalized through the technicist and rationalist approaches adopted by the organizations.

Monitoring was often cited (in both the policy texts and the interviews) as one of the main methods for ensuring that policies were being implemented and for measuring their effectiveness. All the case-study universities had monitoring procedures, usually for student and staff recruitment and selection, either in place or were being put in place. However, a collection of gender and ethnically based statistics is essentially uninformative without a qualitative insight into the equal opportunities process within the organization. While respondents from all the groups tended to state that monitoring was 'essential', a 'crucial tool' for assessing the success of the policies, I was also told that monitoring had either been difficult in terms of actually being able to collect the statistical data or in terms of translating and feeding that data back into the policies. For example, the registrar in Castlebrook University felt that:

> Monitoring is essential and we've put a lot of work into devising monitoring systems for our student intake but we are having problems with it, mainly because black students don't want to fill in the ethnic background categories and we're going to have to look at that carefully. I think perhaps they feel that they don't know why we want to know or how we are going to use it. Even though we clearly state it is only for purposes of monitoring our policies . . . I think people are suspicious.

There was little disclosed recognition of the limitations of monitoring, yet these limitations were inadvertently commented on by some respondents. For example, illustrating the limitations of what monitoring statistics can actually say about how successful the equal opportunities policies are on the ground, the Director of Northfield University told me:

Director: Our monitoring has been effective, we know we have about 50/50 as regards gender in our student body and we know our intake of Asian students has grown, although we still have too few Afro-Caribbean students and we're going to have to do more work on that. But whether it shows that we're implementing our policies is a different question.

SN: In what way?

Director: Implementation of policies is a very complex procedure . . . multi-layered and monitoring can't really always address that but you always need to have that monitoring procedure constantly going on.

Despite the voicing of problems with monitoring, monitoring was over-whelmingly seen as an area that had to be continued to be worked on and refined rather than fundamentally reassessed. In many ways, monitoring appears to be almost a 'red herring' in equal opportunities policy pro-cesses. It appears, or is made to appear, more valuable and important than it actually is. In other words, to be able to point to an extensive monitoring programme bolsters apparent commitment to equal opportunities policies, while monitoring actually represents little more than a passive and technicist procedure. This is not to deny that there isn't a role for the collection of gender or ethnically based statistics, but that there is a need to recognize the limitations of monitoring information in its present quantitative forms. As one academic respondent in Northfield University commented:

Yes I think monitoring is really necessary but it's difficult as well because you don't really need monitoring to tell you there's hardly any black academic staff here or that women are under-represented on the science and technology courses.

An over-reliance on monitoring data can also present dangers in inter-pretation. For example, in Russell College, a monitoring system to assess course failure rate had been introduced. These figures showed that the highest rate of failure came from the African/Caribbean student group and this information was presented (to the Equal Opportunities Committee on which I observed) with little explanatory context. The availability of such information without qualitative information into why this failure may be occurring can, almost inevitably, lead to a reinforcement of racist notions about the abilities of African/Caribbean students in higher education (see Troyna, 1984).

While implementation of equal opportunities in relation to students tended to have been collapsed into monitoring, equal opportunities imple-mentation for staff tended to be collapsed into the terrain of personnel procedures and further marginalized by an over-emphasis on 'fair inter-viewing'. In all the case studies, senior management emphasized that at least one member of any interview panel for staff recruitment would have undergone some form of equal opportunities training. Northfield and Peoples Universities were planning to ensure that all members of staff who were involved in interviewing panels would have undergone equal opportunities training. Yet when I inquired about the nature of this training, this was often explained as learning 'what are the right questions to ask and what aren't the right questions to ask'. There is then a need to avoid the tendency to reduce policy guidelines and policy implementation to a set of technical criteria (Ball, 1994: 8; see also CRE, 1986). Yet the research showed that this tendency had not only *not* been avoided, but that equal opportunities was being actively channelled into these specifically rationalist and technicist directions.

Ease and unease: hierarchies within the equal opportunities paradigm

I noted earlier how patterns of competition emerge through the development of hierarchies between the various groups who have an 'interest' in equality policies (Ouseley, 1990; Anthias and Yuval-Davis, 1992). In terms of exploring whether this same phenomenon occurred in the university case studies part of the research involved a focus on the fragmentation of equal opportunities policies and the configurations of this fragmentation. The notion of hierarchy was employed as a measure of what was 'comfortable' within equal opportunities discourses (reflected in a greater degree of policies/resources/attention) and why and what was 'uncomfortable' (reflected in fewer policies/resources/attention) and why. There was a close correlation between the ways in which the equal opportunities activities of the four universities tended to fragment around particular issues and what aspects of the equal opportunities discourse were seen to be more 'comfortable' and easier to work around. I now examine this fragmentation process by looking at the four most common faces of the equal opportunities rubric.

Gender

Most obviously, a hierarchy had developed within equal opportunities by taking the form of more policies and procedures relating to gender. Gender was the issue which most research respondents felt comfortable discussing and this cut across all four case studies. Gender had a secure place at the top of the equal opportunities hierarchy. Gender had been on the equality agenda in the case-study universities for the longest period of time and this had produced an established policy focus on such issues as maternity provision, job-share, flexi-time, childcare provision, better lighting on campuses and sexual harassment.

There was a familiarity about these issues and the case-study universities all demonstrated a willingness to address and generate policies around these. However, I would argue that this willingness was underpinned by the very nature of the issues, that they can be understood as relating to traditional areas of women's lives – that is, their domestic roles and their need for protection from (outside) sexual violence. For example, at Northfield University, the deputy director told me at some length of his (unsuccessful) efforts to create a well-lit parking space for women members of staff. The advocacy for this initiative on the part of the deputy director and the support it received within the wider university can be understood in its evocation of the need to 'protect' women from 'stranger attacks in the dark'. This was illustrated in my interview with the deputy director: 'I wanted to create a safe haven where women could park all the way through the year *without danger, without fear*' (emphasis added).

Yet, significantly, this concern with women's safety did not generally extend to widespread support for sexual harassment policies. As I noted earlier, in the four case-studies, sexual (and to some extent, racial) harassment policies were perhaps the most contested area of equality policies. Returning to the same interview, the deputy director proceeded to tell me, without any sense of irony or contradiction, of his outrage at 'ridiculous' and 'stupid' campaigns by some women staff to stop the use of the word 'love' as a form of address. This he claimed was 'going too far' and was damaging to the credibility of the 'real' issues which women faced.

Gender was an acceptable aspect of equal opportunities as long as it was approached through non-threatening policies. Positive action was also acceptable as long as it reinforced the domestic divisions of labour and women's vulnerability from 'outside' sexual violence. Hostility to, or doubts about the necessity of, sexual harassment codes and the absence of any positive action policies to increase women's presence in positions of power either in senior management teams or within academic hierarchies is a reflection of this.

A further aspect in maintaining the acceptability of gender rested on the projection of gender as 'white'. In the policy texts and the interviews, there was rarely any recognition of gender being a disparate, fractured category. As I noted earlier, many of those people who had formal responsibility for equal opportunities within the case studies were women, women who almost invariably explained their commitment to equal opportunities in terms of having a primary interest in gender without relating gender to other forms of oppression. For example, the coordinator of the Women's Unit in Northfield University admitted that although she 'would like to see it', there was actually no liaison between the unit and the Racial Equality Centre. The absence of the identification of an interface between gender and race in policy documents and by equal opportunities workers meant that black and other minority ethnic women had effectively been made invisible. If I questioned this invisibility in the interviews with white female respondents, it was not rare for very stereotypical and racist images of black and other minority ethnic women to emerge. The female head of human resources at Castlebrook University told me that:

Many of the Afro-Caribbean women students here are more likely to have dependent children and be single parents, so part of our equal opportunities policy is to have good childcare provision and have things like courses not starting at nine in the morning every day.

Such pathologizing was not confined to African-Caribbean women. Discussing the limited success of various outreach projects which Northfield University had initiated to encourage more South Asian women from the local community to enrol on courses, the university secretary explained:

We've tried to get women from the Asian population here to come in and do part-time study but the culture is that they are not let out if you like. Their husbands and families don't let them out and have very strict rules about their freedom . . . in some racial groups women are treated in a really, really oppressed way, you know, to the point of having an arranged marriage and having to sit at the back of the synagogue or whatever it is . . . they are not treated in . . . not with the same kind of freedoms . . . that makes it very difficult really.

Where black women were visible through their actual presence on the (academic) staff within an institution, they were cast in the role of 'superwomen' – as black women who had reached their position against all odds – and/or they were viewed as 'race experts'. As a black woman lecturer in Peoples University stated:

There are so few black women, we get overwhelmed with work and requests . . . to sit on committees, to speak at forums, to give lectures, to read things . . . course material . . . to make sure it's OK in relation to a race. It does get too much sometimes, but also you feel that you've got to do it, otherwise nobody will.

At Northfield University, a black academic explained how she felt she was treated like 'Some rare kind of exotic creature who did, quotes, "race work" and who it was best not to get close to'.

While gender can be seen as being the comfortable or acceptable area of the equal opportunities paradigm in the case-study universities, this was subject to certain conditions: gender equality policies related to traditional areas of women's lives, that women's needs were seen as homogeneous and that gender was defined as the experience of white women.

Disability

Together with gender, disability was a second area that was rapidly climbing the equal opportunities hierarchy. Disability was increasingly gaining a policy and resource focus. For example, Castlebrook University had produced a separate policy document relating to disability, while gender, race and sexuality were all covered together in the same policy texts. Similarly in Russell College, a Disability Committee had been established in 1991, while it was within the remit of the Equal Opportunities Committee to oversee all other equality issues. Disability was an area which respondents identified as 'easier' to work around: 'People are generally happy to talk about disability, although if there is actually a person with disabilities in the same room, then there is often a lot of embarrassment' (Equal opportunities officer, Russell College).

Like gender, the willingness of an institution to take up and address a disabilities agenda has to be located within that agenda's ability to reinforce certain conceptions about the nature of disability (i.e. dependency) and the needs of disabled people being overwhelmingly physical. That 'embarrassment' emerges when people with disabilities themselves become involved in the policy processes indicates that there are far more complex (political) issues that surround disability (Morris, 1991). However, such issues are submerged under policy processes which centre on concerns around the provision of lifts, ramps, widened doorways, hearing loops, health and safety, etc. For example, although Castlebrook University's disability policy document states in its introduction that the 'University regards disability as an area of equal opportunities', the remainder of the document provides information on the accessibility of the university environment for disabled students and staff (*Enabling You, Students with Disabilities: A Guide to Policy and Procedure*, 1993). Likewise, when I was invited to observe a two-hour meeting of Russell College's Disability Committee, it was given over entirely to a discussion of health and safety measures and requirements for wheelchair users. I am not arguing that these are not valid or necessary areas of attention, but they take place outside of any wider context of discussion about disability and 'ableism'. I would suggest it is for this reason that disability has become an acceptable or 'easy' area of the equal opportunities paradigm.

The research revealed that, in higher education, hierarchies within the equal opportunities community developed according to the ability of the institution to *depoliticize* the categories of equal opportunities. In other words, policy initiatives regarding gender and disability could be reduced to fit most neatly into the classic liberalism of the 'removal of barriers' equal opportunities model, while race and sexuality represent more troublesome and less pliable categories.

Sexuality

Sexuality, (in terms of sexual orientations), had a minimalist presence within the policy documents, tending not to appear beyond mentioning lesbian and gay as categories, against whom discriminatory behaviour was unacceptable (although the events at Russell College illustrate that even this can be problematic; see Chapter 5). If sexuality was mentioned in interviews, it was identified as a 'difficult' area and there was a general reluctance to discuss it. Farish *et al.* (1995: 180) found in their research that respondents would often request that comments made in relation to gay staff be deleted. Sexuality was the only area of equal opportunities in which no rhetorical claims were made as to wanting to see fairer representations of lesbian and gay staff or students, nor did sexuality feature on any monitoring forms. In effect, sexuality was a 'no-go' area on the case-study universities' equal opportunities agendas. This unwillingness to include lesbian and gay issues within equal opportunities policy-making clearly reflects my wider arguments as to the fundamentally depoliticized nature of equality discourses within higher education and the tangential relationship between the equal opportunities policies adopted by higher education institutions and genuine social justice concerns. Any equal opportunities discourse and activity which is based on countering/challenging oppression and domination would automatically have to include the experiences of lesbian and gay people. The absence of, and a reluctance to address, a sexuality dimension in the case-study universities' equal opportunities approaches thereby acts as a (heterosexist) indicator of the limited, non-political scope of those policies.

Race

Race was the area most commonly identified as difficult and uncomfortable. Unlike gender or disability, race is impossible to depoliticize, yet, unlike sexuality, race had a very central presence on the equal opportunities agenda. Probing why respondents perceived race as a more problematic issue than gender, three clearly identifiable themes emerged, which all tended to cast black and minority ethnic groups, rather than racism, as problematic.

The first of these themes was represented in the argument that the institution has a responsibility to provide equality of opportunity, a 'level playing field', but that it could go no further than this. This line was most commonly associated with senior management responses:

> We make sure we've got good access routes, we make sure that the curriculum reflects our multicultural society and we make sure that the racial harassment code is in order. We want to ensure that doors aren't closed for black people but we can't bring about equality of outcome.
> (Vice-Chancellor, Castlebrook University)

The second theme was represented in a 'race is a very complex area' argument. Despite the accuracy of this observation, when this argument surfaced (mainly from respondents in senior management and those formally involved with equal opportunities categories), this complexity was explained in terms of there being 'a lot of racism' between black people themselves. For example, the Pro-Vice-Chancellor of Castlebrook University, who was also chair of the university's Equal Opportunities Committee, went so far as to claim that:

> Actually, the majority of racial problems that we have here tend not to be between white people and black people but between the different cultures, those students who come from different African countries,

but also between our Afro-Caribbean students and our Asian students and that's particularly difficult to deal with.

Similarly, this theme can again be heard in the comments made by the chair of the Race Advisory Group at Northfield University:

> There is such a wide range of issues associated with race, there is inter-racial issues between black and Asian populations, it's such a multiple. With gender it's quite easy because you've just got male and female but with race . . . gender can get people's backs up, but with race . . . it gets people's backs up too but it makes them feel uncomfortable as well.

This invoking of (natural) cultural hostilities not only drew on new racist discourses (Barker, 1981) and deflected attention away from institutional racism, but it also projected the idea that race was an impossible issue for even 'well-meaning' white people to understand and that it was difficult for white people to know what to do about it:

> Some years ago we were trying to get some anti-racist training and we got nowhere because of the difficulties in trying to define what we were actually talking about or wanted when we all sat down. It was quite com-plicated and I think we needed help ourselves in looking at the issues . . . is it about colour or other cultures? So it got quite tricky and we abandoned it and we've never done any anti-racist training or racism awareness. We have a black member of staff now and she is certainly very good at pointing out where certain policies are going to work against black students, so she's pretty good on those sorts of issues.
>
> (Equal opportunities convenor, education faculty,
> Peoples University)

Within this response, it is clearly possible to read the black-expert theme. A presented white uncertainty about how to address race issues or even recognize racist processes can only be alleviated through the guidance and direction of a black person. In this way, race becomes a black responsibility. Directly linked with this 'uncertainty' was the third theme which I widely encountered: the 'fear' theme. By this I mean there was a tendency for white respondents to present themselves as being frightened to even talk about race issues and black people. The idea that white people were frightened of race, of saying the 'wrong thing', of exposing themselves as racist, surfaced numerous times in the interviewing process. The sub-text of this seemed to be that black people and anti-racism had managed to create a code of cultural morality which white people had become terrified of transgressing. For example, the equal opportunities convenor in the personnel depart-ment in Peoples University told me at the end of her interview how she had felt very apprehensive about talking to me about race issues because she didn't feel confident about 'using the right words'. I discussed the fear issue earlier in relation to research dilemmas in Chapter 1 and I argued that this fear has to be linked to the wider context of racist ideology. In the white imagination, fear of black people – the rapist, the mugger, the primitive – has been a key element in the construction of racism. That the 'fear' expressed by white respondents in relation to race goes much deeper and is more complex than just uncertainty about using the 'right' words was demonstrated in my interview with the chair of the Race Advisory Group at Northfield University (a white male dean). This respondent emotionally recalled an incident in which he had been invited to speak at a forum about black women in business:

> It was a *petrifying experience* and I made a complete fool of myself. There were black women talking about their experiences and then when it was my turn to speak . . . I was stupid to accept the invitation . . . I introduced myself as a white man and that was a bad statement to make because it immediately discriminated against everyone else who was black and female – so I'd exposed my own racism. It made me extremely *uncomfortable*. I couldn't excuse it, I had no other excuse than that I was *petrified* and didn't know what to do. *I think that's what people feel when their racism is exposed* (emphasis added).

What seems to be being relayed here is a rather ironical and contradictory situation in which a powerful white male is terrified by his contact with a number of black women. As I explored in Chapter 1, what was also interesting in these situations was the role in which I was cast, as some form of 'expert' who, despite being white, knew, by virtue of the type of questions that I was asking, the 'right things to say'. Increasingly I came to see this presentation of 'fear' as a form of almost cathartic 'confessionalism'. The concern with 'saying the right thing' actually served as an excuse for not 'saying the right thing' but, more fundamentally, it served to stop race and racism being thought about or talked about in any real or meaningful way within the case studies and this was reflected in the limited amount of tangible commitment that was given to tackling race issues.

In the case studies, the attempts to depoliticize race, to make it more comfortable by boxing it into categories of access, multicultural curriculum, monitoring and racial harassment codes had been only partially successful. My explorations into why (white) respondents found race difficult or uncomfortable illustrated the extent to which race continued to seep out of such technicist and rationalist approaches and maintain a contested and political profile which bubbled just below the surfaces of the equality discourses within the case studies.

Because of the need to contain it in this position, race had been exiled to the peripheries of the equal opportunities agenda. The clearest example of this was presented by Northfield University, where despite having quite extensive structures in place to address 'racial equality' – a Racial Equality Centre, a Race Advisory Committee, equal opportunities workers – race remained in the foothills of the equal opportunities hierarchy. This situation was openly acknowledged by senior management in the university:

Policy development has been far more difficult in this organization and yet we've had special funding to fund the Racial Equality Centre . . . *I don't know why it is,* all I know is that it's been more difficult to get policy development on race . . . always. Race policy has lagged behind gender policy and yet we have many more structures doing the work . . . *the issues are more difficult.* I think you can treat gender issues in a homogeneous way, you can say all women experience similar kinds of discrimination but I don't think you can say the same is true with all the different racial groups.

(University secretary, emphasis added)

Such a response exposes the way in which race is conceived as representing 'a can of worms' and as being too 'complex and incomprehensible', and is considered within a 'what more can we do' argument, rather than being approached within a serious conceptual and policy framework.

Conclusion

This chapter has explored what happens to equal opportunities policies in the everyday world of the case-study universities. The chapter has used the data gained by interviewing those responsible for equal opportunities policy-making and policy implementation to argue that there were certain processes at work which acted to constrain and limit the effectiveness of those policies. These processes were: the narrow, managerial ownership of equality policies, the marginalization of equality structures and equality questions, and the hierarchical development of 'comfortable/uncomfortable' categories within equal opportunities discourses. The chapter seeks to suggest that the responses that the case-study universities made towards equal opportunities were only loosely linked to genuine concerns of social justice. There was little evidence in the case studies that the universities had taken any positive lessons from earlier attempts by other organizations (most notably local authorities) in their generation and implementation of equality policies, or that the policy processes incorporated reflexive or self-critical dimensions (Chapter 4). If any lessons had been taken at all, the research suggests these were negative ones, reflected in a desire to avoid contentious or difficult areas of equal opportunities and reduce questions of equality and related approaches to a set of mechanical, technicist and rationalist criteria. In other words, in the 'equiphobic', politically correct climate of the 1990s, the case-study universities' willingness to address an equal opportunities agenda depended on their ability to depoliticize the issues involved. Although there may have been a few solitary (academic) voices of radicalism in the case studies who were prepared to offer a more political reading of equal opportunities, these were very much on the sidelines of the policy processes.

In a higher education system that is based on competitive individualism and an achievement hierarchy, the aim of reconstructing this system in terms of equability (or even parity) is not seriously seen to be possible or, in effect, desirable (Troyna and Williams, 1986: 107). The central questions are not simply access to higher education, the numerical presence of previously excluded groups or the mobility of black people or women in terms of acquisition of higher educational credentials, but the nature of hierarchy within higher education itself (Gundara, 1983; see Chapter 2). The following chapter considers the role(s) that the local AUT and NATFHE associations took in relation to quality policies in the university case studies.

6

Academic Trade Union Responses to Equality Policies

Introduction

While equal opportunities issues had secured a place within the case-study universities, as Chapters 4 and 5 have shown, this place was both contested and ambiguous in the everyday world of the institutions. In effect, equality discourses and policies constituted an 'arena of struggle' (Ball, 1987: 115). This chapter examines the ways in which the AUT and NATFHE have entered this arena of struggle. The central focus is on the positions that these two academic trade unions took up in relation to equal opportunities policies in the case-study universities.

The chapter begins by discussing the equal opportunities policy texts that the AUT and NATFHE have each developed at a national level, and what recommendations these texts make for local union associations. Then I examine the equal opportunities activity of the AUT and NATFHE within the four case-study universities – was there any such activity, what forms did this activity take and how did union officials interpret their relationship with equality issues? The third area the chapter concentrates on is how senior management and formal and informal equal opportunities activists viewed the positions taken up by the AUT and NATFHE in relation to the equal opportunities agenda – did these respondents see academic trade unions as having a specific equal opportunities role and responsibility?

Documentation

The AUT

Between 1984 and 1991, the AUT produced a number of policy statements: *Ensuring Equal Opportunities for University Staff and Students from Ethnic Minorities* (1987); *Sexual Orientation and Employment in the Universities* (1990); *Equal Opportunities: A Code of Practice for the Employment of Women in Universities*

(1984); *Sexual Harassment: Code of Practice and Procedure for Individual Case Studies* (1985); and also for gender, *Negotiating Pack for Positive Action* (1985). There were a number of spin-off documents which were concerned with gender issues. These concerns covered the standardized areas of maternity and/or dependency leave, job-share and flexi-time, nursery provision and childcare facilities, safety and security, and extended into recruitment and career development, promotion and training. In terms of equal opportunities, the AUT was commonly associated by the research respondents with a commitment to gender and women's issues. This association was buttressed by the triennial publication of *AUT Woman*, which has been distributed to every (male and female) AUT member since 1983. While I will return to these policies on gender, I want to now focus on the *Ensuring Equal Opportunities for University Staff and Students from Ethnic Minorities* (EEOUSSEM) policy document. In May 1987, the AUT Council, the union's supreme decision-making body, passed the following resolution:

> Council endorses the policy statement *Ensuring Equal Opportunities for Staff and Students from Ethnic Minorities* as a positive contribution to the protection of the rights of ethnic minority staff and students and to the encouragement of their participation in all aspects of University life. *Council calls on Local Associations to make every effort to secure the adoption and implementation of the policy statement in their institutions.*
> (EEOUSSEM, 1987: i; emphasis added)

The content of the policy document and the style in which it is written reflects a mixture of liberal and radical perspectives and has a much more overtly political edge to it than similar documents produced by the case-study universities. For example, the document contains a relatively lengthy introduction setting out why there is a need for the policy. In this it initially evokes a strongly integrationist theme: 'our universities have an important part to play in the promotion of understanding of and respect for different ethnic and cultural attributes' and argues, 'education to degree level is now a minimum qualification for entry into to a wide range of professions. The presence of members of ethnic minority groups in positions of professional and political importance in our society is a *key aspect of their struggle for acceptance*' (EEOUSSEM, 1987: 1; emphasis added). Yet despite recognizing that 'British society is permeated by racist attitudes and behaviour', the document immediately proceeds to state that it is higher education's 'colour blindness' and not racism that has been responsible for racial inequality:

> to point out that there are aspects of the university system that result in inequality of opportunity and racial prejudice is not to accuse universities of direct or intentional discrimination; to do so would be to *misunderstand the nature of racism* and the ways in which it manifests itself in education.
> (EEOUSSEM, 1987: 1; emphasis added)

There are important silences in the EEOUSSEM document. The terms 'black' and 'anti-racism' are not referred to (see Chapter 6) and the language of the document is dominated by the terms 'ethnic minorities', 'racial discrimination' and 'race relations' (a glossary of these is provided at the end of the document). In my interview with a senior national AUT official, this apparent reluctance to invoke 'anti-racism' in the policy text was combined with an unwillingness to accuse universities of racist practice, as the following excerpt from the transcript illustrates:

> *SN*: Anti-racism specifically doesn't seem to come up in the policy documents . . .

> *Senior AUT official*: I would not actually attach the label anti-racism to the work that we're doing to encourage ethnic minorities into universities. There is a subtle difference because anti-racism implies that there is a positive campaign against ethnic minorities. I don't think there is. I just think that it is out of ignorance rather than ill will . . . and because of the *lack of applications* across the spectrum in universities and, of course, there is also the *problem of the number of ethnic minority students coming through who are the right calibre* (emphasis added).

Besides the unwillingness to employ the term 'anti-racism', the defining of racism as 'ill will', the shifting of responsibility onto black and other minority ethnic people ('lack of applications') and the implied scarcity of academically able black and other minority ethnic students are all significant in this response.

Drawing heavily on the CRE's (1984) Code of Practice, the EEOUSSEM document details the legislative framework (Race Relations Act, 1976) for racial equality and the type of action which universities should be taking in relation to ensuring this. While these recommendations follow the prescribed and familiar route which is common to the policy texts formulated by the universities themselves – the adoption of an equal opportunities statement, monitoring and the collection of ethnically based statistics, reviewing recruitment, interviewing, selection, training and promotion procedures, and developing a racial harassment code – the document also advocates a number of trade union based initiatives. These include AUT cooperation with the introduction, generation and implementation of equal opportunities policies. If monitoring shows that discrimination has occurred or is occurring, then the AUT should cooperate in measures to eliminate this and should encourage management to develop positive action programmes where there is under-representation of black and other minority ethnic groups. If management itself has introduced such programmes, then unions should fully support these (EEOUSSEM, 1987: 12–13).

In making these recommendations, the AUT clearly placed upon its local associations, a particular role and responsibility for equal opportunities issues within universities. The EEOUSSEM document identifies not simply a supportive role but rather an initiating and pro-active role. For example, in terms of policy implementation structures, the EEOUSSEM document urges universities to allocate responsibility for equality issues to a senior member of staff (i.e. to create an equal opportunities adviser/officer post) and recommends that a similar position is taken on by a member of each local association:

A fairly senior member of the university's administration should be allocated special responsibility for overseeing a programme of action for ethnic minority staff and the campus trade union should nominate someone to perform an equivalent function from its side. It is essential that both individuals receive at least basic training in race relations practice.

(EEOUSSEM, 1987: 14)

While both Peoples University and Russell College had created equal opportunity adviser/officer posts, there had been no equivalent position created by the local AUT associations in these universities, and neither the equal opportunities director at Peoples University nor the equal opportunities officer at Russell College worked closely (or at all) with the AUT on equality issues generally and certainly not race issues in particular. This theme, the space between nationally made policy and local union activity, is one to which I shall return later in the chapter.

As I noted above, in terms of equal opportunities the AUT is widely associated (and associates itself) with having been committed to its women members and gender inequality in higher education. The majority of documents to which I was given access related to gender issues and, as I noted above, they tended to be concerned with very prescribed areas, echoing the technicism and rationalism of the policy texts developed within the case-study universities. Unlike the EEOUSSEM document, the gender policy texts were much more standardized and, apart from the most extensive document, a *Negotiating Pack of Positive Action* (1985), contained no contextualizing introductions as to the need for such policies, nor did any of the documents contain glossaries explaining the terms used. In contrast to the racial equality policy document, the gender equality texts appeared as non-contested and unpolitical. The gender documents also differed from the EEOUSSEM policy document in that they did not directly cite local union responsibility for ensuring gender equality initiatives. For example, the gender documents did not urge the local associations to select a specific representative to liaise with senior management and oversee the implementation of a gender equality programme.

The main difference between the AUT policy documents relating to gender and the universities' gender equality documents was the emphasis that the AUT placed on positive action. The *Negotiating Pack of Positive Action* (1985) was designed as a detailed positive action guide for the local associations and covered a variety of areas around recruitment, promotion, career development, conditions of service and working conditions as they relate specifically to women members of staff. The pack made a number of overall recommendations for planning and implementing a positive action strategy. These recommendations included the establishment of women's committees within each local association, advised that AUT members ought to serve on universities equal opportunities committees and, where these did not exist, recommended pressure for the creation of such a committee. The pack generally urged local associations to 'spearhead' equal opportunities campaigns and to seek to influence the decision-making structures within individual higher education institutions.

Generally, the AUT's equal opportunities policy texts emphasized that local associations have a campaigning and pro-active role, should create their own equal opportunities structures – an adviser on race and women's committees – and use the wider union body to both influence and be a voice in their universities' equal opportunities policy processes.

NATFHE

As with the AUT, NATFHE had developed a number of equal opportunities policy documents. The main policy texts included a *NATFHE Against Racism* (1986) resource pack, which included a statement of anti-racism and strategies for action for the union to combat racism and a summary of the 1976 Race Relations Act, and *NATFHE Action Against Sexist or Racist Harassment: Branch Guidelines* (1986). There were also policy documents relating to 'traditional' gender issues in further and higher education (job-share, maternity leave, flexi-time, child-care) and women's participation in NATFHE (*Breaking Down the Barriers*, 1981; *Time for a New Initiative*, 1984). NATFHE had addressed sexuality issues, reflected in the *Sexual Orientation Discussion Paper* (1986) and more recently had written an *Equal Opportunities Language Guide* (1993).

As with the AUT equality policy documents, NATFHE's equal opportunities texts had a more political edge to them than those produced by the case-study universities. For example, while the *NATFHE Against Racism* (1986) resource pack provided a summary of the 1976 Race Relations Act, it also urged that 'All members should accept their individual responsibility as well as their collective responsibility for opposing racism' (p. 5). The document made a number of recommendations for local branches:

> Branches should seek to ensure that college policies are adopted and implemented, including a multicultural and anti-racist curriculum and the creation of a post/posts . . . with responsibility for monitoring the implementation of [such] policies.
>
> Branches should establish with management proper college procedures for reporting on and dealing with racist or allegedly racist material brought on to college premises and ensure that these procedures are widely known. Branches should consider the appointment of a member responsible for monitoring these [equality] policies.
>
> (pp. 5–6)

The *NATFHE Against Racism* document places a clear emphasis on local union associations' responsibility for race issues and identifies a role for NATFHE in relation to equality policy processes within individual universities. However, in an interview with a senior NATFHE official, I was told that there were difficulties in the uptake of national policy at a local level: 'What is sent to association secretaries is usually lost or ignored . . . there are some secretaries who are not sympathetic to equal opportunities issues but more often it is the time factor which restricts activity in the area'.

The emphasis on local union responsibility for equal opportunities in the national NATFHE policy documentation shares with the AUT and individual universities' equal opportunities policies, a technicist orientation. Technicist strategies such as appointing local union members with special responsibility for equality issues were much in evidence in NATFHE's equal opportunities policy texts. For example, the *NATFHE Action Against Sexist or Racist Harassment: Branch Guidelines* (1988) stated that 'it is the responsibility of the Branch to ensure that there is one officer responsible for receiving complaints of harassment' (p. 4). Similarly, the *Breaking Down the Barriers* (1981) and *Time for a New Initiative* (1984) documents both urged the creation of local women's committees as a way of increasing both women's participation in NATFHE and prioritizing 'women's issues' within further and higher education institutions.

What is clear from the national equal opportunities policy texts of both the AUT and NATFHE is the advocation of local associations' involvement with the equal opportunities policy-making and implementation processes in universities. However, the recommended forms for this involvement fall within a technicist and mechanical policy framework of committees, specialist posts and advisers. The technicism of both unions' equal opportunities policy texts and the lack of self-criticism, reflexivity and evaluation obscured the wider questions as to academic unions' responsibilities regarding the issues of social justice within higher education.

Local AUT and NATFHE responses to equal opportunities

Inaction and apathy: Russell College

In only one of the case-study universities, Russell College, was there any formal representation of either the AUT and NATFHE in university equal opportunities structures. Russell College had reserved a place for an AUT representative (selected by the local association) on its Equal Opportunities Committee. That there was an absence of such conventional and minimal forms of union involvement in three of the four case studies was immediately significant as an indicator of either unions' exclusion or inactivity in the equality arena. Neither was there any formal AUT or NATFHE representation in any of the other equal opportunities structures in place in the case-study universities. In Northfield University and Peoples University where, as Chapter 5 has discussed, there were more extensive structures in which union involvement of some form may have been expected, this too was absent.

Within the national equal opportunities policy documents of both the AUT and NATFHE, there had been clear recommendations that local associations should create their own women's committees and race equality advisers to work with senior management in supporting and/or encouraging initiatives in these areas (see above). Yet none of the four branches studied had, at the time of the research, any such structures. Significantly, all four case-study universities had had women's committees during the 1980s, but these had drifted and eventually fizzled out during the early 1990s. As with the development of national equality policies during the early to mid-1980s, the one-time existence of these women's committees appeared to correlate to the period in which equal opportunities discourses and initiatives were in the ascendancy on (some) municipal agendas and generally had a higher public profile. However, even during this time, the four local associations had never created the special advisory positions in relation to race equality.

Despite this general picture of inactivity on the part of the AUT and NATFHE, the (former) AUT representative on the Equal Opportunities Committee at Russell College argued that the AUT had been responsible for initiating an equal opportunities agenda within the university:

> The AUT pressed equal opportunities quite strongly here. I think it's really the work that we've done that led to the Equal Opportunities Committee and the other things being set up . . . it was really the pressure of the unions here that got equal opportunities rolling.

However, this claim was contradicted by the university's personnel officer, whose brief specifically covered staff and equal opportunities and who was also a representative on the Equal Opportunities Committee:

> It [the AUT] seems to choose to take other issues, like pay, to put its energies into. But having said that, when issues are raised, then the AUT is certainly not hostile – sadly it doesn't initiate, maybe it shouldn't, it's not necessarily their role, but I think that sometimes it's nice, particularly for management to hear trade unions knocking on the door and asking uncomfortable questions about equal opportunities issues. Women have come up sometimes but I have never heard the AUT or any other of the unions on campus ask anything about race . . . never.

Probing this contradiction I questioned the association secretary about the difficulties in implementing national AUT equal opportunities guidelines at a local level. This respondent demonstrated an uncertainty as to what these guidelines actually were:

> I know that the AUT has done some work in that area . . . but . . . offhand I can't recall particular policies. Obviously equal opportunities is

something we would be supportive of . . . on several occasions we've tried to persuade the university to say that it is an equal opportunities employer in its advertising but it has always preferred to say 'working towards equal opportunities'. Quite what the difference is who knows?

This response offers a curious mixture of positions between seeing equal opportunities as an area in which the AUT should, ideally, have involvement, but this is mediated by a lack of energy and political will in terms of making this involvement active. Questioning in the same interview ways in which the AUT could become more engaged with equal opportunities issues in the university, the respondent stated that: 'In principle, no-one in the association would object to more involvement I'm sure, it's just a question of anybody being prepared to find time to do it . . . we really do operate at a minimalist level here'.

The degree of apathy that surfaced here did not appear to arise from actual hostility or an oppositional position towards equal opportunities issues, but more from an inability to generate activity around, or channel energy into, raising the profile of equality issues. For example, in my interview with the association treasurer, I questioned whether gender or race had been priority areas which the association had targeted and if women and black members participated in the association:

SN: Is self-organization, as in say a women's or a black members' committee, a strategy which the AUT would consider here?

AT: I'm never terribly sure about caucuses. Here am I, a white middle-class male, and caucuses look . . . I'm indifferent I think . . . if the people concerned definitely think it's useful, then I take the fairly wimpish view that who am I to say that they're wrong, but I do worry that they're divisive and ghettoist.

SN: So has there ever been any such committees?

AT: Well there was one some years ago, there was a women's committee, but *I don't know if there still is.* I certainly don't remember there being any hostility to it (emphasis added).

Besides this absence of awareness as to whether his own association actually still had a women's committee, what is also interesting here is the abdication of responsibility on the part of the association treasurer. Being 'a white middle-class male' is an identity that is invoked to situate himself outside of equality discourses and justifies both his indifference (although it is clear that he veers towards opposing the notion of caucuses/self-organization) and his 'who am I to say they're wrong' position.

This 'mood' of apathy and indifference towards equality issues pervaded my interviews with AUT officials in Russell College. In my interview with the AUT representative on the university's Equal Opportunities Committee, she explained her position in the following terms:

I am interested in women and gender but really I only took the representative job because nobody else wanted to take it on at the time ... I'm not that sure what I should be doing because I don't know much about what goes on with the [equal opportunities] committee. The association wants me to report back from meetings and I would like to be more pro-active but it's difficult. Doing a full-time job and then union work and we're [association] pretty busy right now ... I don't think I'll do it [be the representative] next year.

Although apathy and inaction emerged as the dominant themes in relation to equal opportunities in Russell College, apathy and inaction characterized the association as a whole. The association had a low profile within Russell College generally. Even tracking down the local union officials was not immediately straightforward. I had to ask a number of respondents, many of whom, despite being AUT members, did not know who their union representatives were, before I was able to identify the association officials. In a revealing comment made by the association's treasurer in response to my question as to the university management's attitude to the AUT, he told me that:

AT: Sometimes they [management] go ahead and do things without consulting us. Sometimes we do negotiate and lose the argument and sometimes we persuade them, talk to them, whatever. But I am surprised that they don't actually bluntly say 'we know how weak the association is and we're going to take no notice whatsoever'. Obviously that would be very confrontational and would cause bad feeling and all the rest of it, but I can't see our membership taking to the streets or actually doing much.

SN: Why?

AT: Well I think management could do it partly because the membership is so apathetic and partly because so many people are on short-term contracts now.

The AUT at Russell College was clearly located on the very peripheries of the institution. For the staff, membership of the union went no further than the membership itself and the minimalism of the association was reinforced by the apathy and inaction of its local leadership. The central and most recent concerns of the association were short-term contracts and pay. In other words, the main issue which the association had prioritized was in the very traditional area of conditions of service and defending union members. However, while the AUT in Russell College identified its priorities in traditional trade union terms, it was also anxious not to present itself as operating in what it saw as traditional trade union ways:

Defending our members yes, but not bigotly or blindly ... which makes it difficult to see it [the AUT] as a *real trade union*. There is a managerial feel to it. There are very few members here, in fact I can't really

think of any, who take what you would call a hard trade union position
and if there were they would definitely stand out.

(Association secretary, emphasis added)

What is interesting here is the direct distancing of the AUT from the
wider trade union movement and the evocation of the AUT as having a
different political character (i.e. having a 'managerial feel'). This is an
important point. The 'managerial feel' of the AUT, if this does exist,
has to be attributed to factors other than simply the vertical recruitment
patterns of the AUT: although members of senior management teams
are often members of the AUT, as they were in both Russell College and
Peoples University, this alone is not sufficient to influence the total political
character of a union (see Prandy *et al.*, 1983).

My research into a local association of the AUT in Russell College presented me with a micro picture of the union in which its most prevalent
features were its peripheral location in the everyday world of the university
and its apathy/inactivity around equal opportunities issues. Yet, in many
ways, as significant as these findings were, the insights that I received in
relation to the more general political character of the AUT, as articulated
through a definition of its primary role and responsibility to defend its
members and the notion that the AUT differed from 'real trade unions',
were more revealing. This latter idea can also be traced back to the debates
in the 1970s as to whether the AUT should affiliate to the TUC, thus
adopting a union identity rather than a professional association identity. It
is significant that twenty years after TUC affiliation, there are still voices in
the AUT, albeit at a local and micro level, which dissent from that union
identity and the (working) class associations that go with it.

Inactivity and hostility: Peoples University and Northfield University

While the AUT in Russell College did not demonstrate any particular hostility towards the area of equal opportunities, local union officials in Peoples
University and Northfield University tended to take a more oppositional
approach to equality issues. Unlike Russell College, in Peoples University
the AUT had no formal representation in any of its equal opportunities
structures. Significantly, such involvement was not viewed as necessary or
desirable:

We are not involved with equal opportunities at all. There used to be
one or two members who were active in that area but as a branch we
don't play any particular role in equal opportunities. The university
has the [equal opportunities] unit and it [the unit] has the [equal
opportunities] director and the other staff, and since that all seems
to be working well it doesn't seem *worthwhile* to put our scarce resources

into working on that [equal opportunities]. We are not terribly pro-
active, we don't go out looking for work because just keeping up with
what the university's up to is enough for us to do.

(Association secretary, emphasis added)

This response appeared to summarize the central attitude of the association
towards the whole area of equal opportunities. This central attitude can be
understood as being made up of a number of combined rationales:

- That because the university has established a body which has direct responsibility for equal opportunities policies and issues in the institution,
then there is nothing that the union needs to do.
- That the association is not very active anyway.
- That the association has a large enough workload as it is.

The existence of the Equal Opportunities Unit is used to validate the
total abdication of any responsibility that a local association has for equal
opportunities. The language employed by the association secretary is also
relevant: the idea that it would not be 'worthwhile' for the association to be
active or invest in areas of equal opportunities is particularly significant.
Within such a perspective, equal opportunities is judged as being *outside* of
the jurisdiction of union activity. The following excerpt from the same
interview transcript demonstrates this approach:

SN: Are you satisfied with the participation of women and black members in the branch?

AS: Well we certainly don't have equal numbers on the executive, we
have more men but that doesn't bother me and we don't have any
blacks [*sic*], there aren't many blacks around the campus . . . there are
very few black members of staff . . . you could probably count them on
one hand. I don't know why that is.

SN: Well does the branch have any formal or informal contact with the
Black Staff Group?

AS: No.

SN: Would the branch look to develop such links in the future then?

AS: I think it's more if *they* came to us than us going out to *them*. As
I say, I actually have enough to do without looking for yet more work
to do. We don't go out looking for issues (emphasis added).

What is being stated here goes much further than a position of apathy.
Not only are the needs of black members and the issues of race not seen
as an area in which the union has to concern itself, but it is an area which
the union would not want to concern itself with. This position was also
echoed, albeit more ambiguously, in the response of the vice-president of

the AUT at Peoples University to the idea of making links with the university's Black Staff Group:

> If it was appropriate, if there was a request from that group, then I'm sure the AUT would not not want to . . . we would not say this is not anything we should get involved with . . . but it hasn't cropped up. There are very few black staff. It would be interesting to know how they feel about whether we are looking after them. I don't know whether we are.

This is a curious reply. Stating (rather oddly) that the AUT 'would not not want' to develop a line of liaison with the university's Black Staff Group almost seems to imply that there may be questions about whether the association actually would want such links and the 'if it was appropriate' preface reinforces this impression. Also, it is very clear that any such initiative would have to come out of the Black Staff Group approaching the union rather than the union taking on such a responsibility. There is a paternalistic element to the phrase 'looking after' black members (as opposed to, say, commenting on whether the union is tackling racism). Similarly, the vice-president's own conclusion of not knowing whether the union actually is meeting the needs of that particular membership indicates both a lack of activity and/or concern around race and anti-racism and the absence of any form of communication with black staff in the university.

This apparent unwillingness to address the issue of race extended, in the form of more overt reservations, to other areas of equal opportunities. The university's sexual harassment code was an area in which the association secretary openly expressed opposition:

> I feel that the sexual harassment policy has been taken to extremes by some women. It seems to me that some people may be taking advantage of the policy and I do worry about it, but it would be very difficult for me to take that up as an issue because you would be seen as trying to water down the sexual harassment policy and some of my female colleagues here would not take kindly to it. But I do think we have to worry about how the person who the allegation is made against feels . . . While I'm in favour of people not being sexually harassed at work, I'm also in favour of people having some sort of leeway and not being jumped all over and hauled off in front of management.

A number of themes are being incorporated here: that the policy represents an 'extreme' position; that 'some people may be taking advantage of it'; sympathy for the person whom the complaint is being made against; and the aligning of the policy with management interests ('hauled off in front of management'). Union hostility to sexual harassment codes can also be read as an expression of hostility to equal opportunities policies more widely in terms of a link being made between equality policies and political extremism, and an interpretation of equality policies being management-generated.

This position was similarly reflected at Northfield University, where the local NATFHE union officials condemned sexual harassment policies but also challenged the validity of the whole equal opportunities rubric. As at Peoples University, NATFHE at Northfield University played no part in the university's equal opportunities structures. As with the AUT at Peoples University, NATFHE officials at Northfield University shared the perception that equality issues were not only disconnected with union activities but were also damaging to those union activities. For example, the branch secretary stated:

> We've never been asked to make a representation on the committees or anything like that and we've never asked if we can. Conditions of service and pay have been the big areas that we're constantly involved with as a union. All we ever seem to here about from [NATFHE] head-quarters is equal opportunities, but we've got our hands full with dealing with things like short-term contracts and pay. Nobody ever asks about what we think about all the equal opportunities policies and the policies for women that NATFHE has nationally . . . you're the first person that's ever come to me as a local NATFHE official and asked me what I think about it.

Besides the assertion that NATFHE officials would not ask to be involved in the university's equal opportunities structures, what particularly stands out in this response is the opposition to NATFHE as a national union addressing equality issues. The argument here is that in taking this position, NATFHE nationally is out of touch with the 'real' (traditional) trade union concerns. The notion that there are areas in which a trade union should be active and areas, such as equal opportunities, that are basically outside of a local union's remit, similarly surfaced in my interview with the Negotiating Secretary of the NATFHE branch at Northfield University:

> The university now has numerous people, committees and units which have responsibility for equal opportunities policies, people who do it full-time and are paid to do that. The union here has a responsibility to look after *all* of its members' needs and we as officials can only do so much . . . we've got to look after the other issues . . . the ones that affect the *whole* membership and the ones that only the union is keep-ing an eye on. We can't do everything (emphasis added).

The language of 'all members' and the 'whole membership' is significant and reminiscent of older trade union approaches to black workers and women workers – that is, a colour- and gender-blind approach which refuses to recognize specific and different experiences and needs within the work-place. As we have seen in Chapter 3, the wider trade union movement has attempted to re-position itself on this since the late 1970s and certainly during the 1980s, although as the most recent commentators in the field have noted, these attempts have only been partially successful (GLC, 1984; Lee, 1984; Wrench, 1989, 1992; CRE, 1992; Virdee and Grint, 1994).[1] NATFHE officials in Northfield University demonstrated the extent to which these older colour- and gender-blind approaches still exist within the trade union imagination:

> Well, the NATFHE branch would oppose any form of unfair discrimina-
> tion, there's no doubt in my mind about that, but once you start separ-
> ating the issues out and have women's committees and minorities'
> committees and special advisers . . . well it gets complicated and people
> begin to feel excluded and I'm not sure how much you achieve with
> any of it anyway. But it's never been asked for here.
>
> (Branch treasurer)

At Northfield University, NATFHE's relationship with equal opportunities was expressed through a discourse which alternated between indifference and overt hostility. As at Peoples University, it was Northfield University's sexual harassment initiatives which aroused the most openly hostile union reactions. That these initiatives were 'going too far' was a common response on the part of union officials. Significantly, NATFHE officials appeared to view the university's sexual harassment strategies as a system devised by senior management through which to control and extend its powers over members of staff:

> It's very difficult for the union. Someone makes a complaint and the
> whole thing is immediately in the hands of the sexual harassment
> officer and the director and the disciplinary machinery grinds into
> action and it's people's careers that we're talking about and mud
> sticks . . . have you seen the Code? You can make a complaint and it
> can be more-or-less anything – just a comment – that shouldn't have
> been said perhaps, but you're tried in a kangaroo court and we have
> to defend a union member and it's very difficult in that situation.
> Often there's no proof, just one person's word against another and it's
> management making the decisions.
>
> (Branch secretary)

For the union officials at Northfield University, the sexual harassment initiatives represented the thin end of the wedge of 'politically correct' lunacy:

> Of course women shouldn't be sexually harassed or made to feel un-
> comfortable at work, although it isn't always just women as everybody
> seems to think – it does happen the other way around too, but you
> never hear about that . . . I think it has gone too far here. It's like the
> language guide, it creates a climate of fear. People are afraid of saying
> the wrong thing or of their remarks being misinterpreted and then
> losing their jobs or having their names on a secret list somewhere,
> because that's what you're supposed to do – keep a record and you
> might not know anything about it. It's a form of extremism and the
> union's stuck in the middle of it all.
>
> (Branch treasurer)

It is significant that NATFHE union officials did not appear to envisage themselves as being in a position where they would be supporting a NATFHE member who was actually making a complaint of sexual harassment, although NATFHE national policy guidelines recommend that such a supportive position should be taken (*NATFHE Action Against Sexist or Racist Harassment: Branch Guidelines*, 1986).

As with AUT officials in Peoples University, the hostility that NATFHE officials at Northfield University demonstrated towards the university's sexual harassment policies can be understood as representing opposition to, and suspicion of, equality policies more generally. This can be seen, for example, both in the branch treasurer's references to Northfield University's language guide and in the language this respondent used – 'climate of fear', 'secret lists', 'forms of extremism'.

The position that NATFHE union officials at Northfield University had taken up was one that was at odds with both national NATFHE policy recommendations and with the university's own equal opportunities initiatives. As with the AUT officials in Peoples University, NATFHE officials at Northfield University approached the equal opportunities agenda with suspicion and hostility. Opposition to the wider equality agenda was most obviously expressed through hostility to sexual harassment policies specifically. It is significant that the suspicion with which local union officials, in both these case studies, viewed the equal opportunities paradigm in higher education stemmed in part from their perception that equal opportunities represented management policies and thereby constituted a form of attack on the majority of members of university staff (i.e. those staff members who were not female, black, disabled or gay or lesbian). That equal opportunities policies 'belonged' to senior university management was a theme that similarly emerged in Castlebrook University.

Inaction and exclusion: Castlebrook University

The NATFHE branch in Castlebrook University differed from the local unions in the other case studies in that the branch had union officials who openly expressed both support and commitment to equal opportunities and equality issues. Castlebrook University had only very minimalist equal opportunities structures and there was no formal or informal NATFHE representation or involvement in these. However, local union officials explained this non-representation in terms of exclusion rather than inactivity. For example, the NATFHE branch secretary at Castlebrook University explained how:

> The union has no involvement nor has it been consulted by this [equal opportunities] committee. *As far as equal opportunities is concerned, it belongs to them* [senior management] . . . I mean I only got this new equal opportunities document last week. It's just ridiculous, it's just an

edict from above. I think senior management regard certain things as *being in their gift and equal opportunities has become one of those things* (emphasis added).

While what is being voiced here echoes the local union discourse of senior management 'ownership' of equality initiatives found in Peoples and Northfield Universities, union officials at Castlebrook were critical of this process of management colonization rather than of equal opportunities *per se*. The following excerpt from the same interview transcript illustrates this:

> *BS*: Increasingly, they [equal opportunities] are not even seen as trade union issues, they are becoming much more issues that management are allowed to take the initiative on and I think we [NATFHE] have to be very careful . . .
>
> *SN*: Has this been a deliberate strategy?
>
> *BS*: Well I don't know how deliberate you can say it is, in the way that you mean . . . but I do think that there is a hostility here to letting the union have any say whatever in policies. There is that barrier and I can only conclude that the reason for that is because they [management] do regard these type of issues as being theirs and anything that opens it all up into a wider, more democratic forum is just no-no, like in a private company.

What stands out here in particular is a position which directly identifies equal opportunities issues as trade union issues. Unlike the local unions in the other case-study universities, NATFHE officials at Castlebrook shared an approach which locates the equal opportunities agenda within the remit of trade union activity:

> I do feel that the equal opportunities initiatives that are around, or that have just arrived from above, are cosmetic and it comes back to us in the union because if we're not aware and challenging these things, who will be? I feel that very strongly. Real changes will only happen if there is concerted pressure from below, from unions in particular . . . they represent the workforce and need to be actively involved in this, to have channels to negotiate.
>
> (Branch chair)

However, despite these pro equal opportunities positions, there was virtually no equal opportunities related activity or involvement on the part of NATFHE in Castlebrook University. Probing this contradiction, union officials interpreted this lack of activity in part as exclusion from a process dominated by senior management, but they also explained it in terms of wider issues and a degree of 'slippage' that had occurred in relation to the priority given to the equal opportunities agenda in both the university and NATFHE generally:

I'd be the first to admit that we've let it [equal opportunities] go for a while and that was wrong . . . in union terms we're [branch officials] the voice of the union, but because we've been so busy just running the union, we've neglected some of those basic issues, equality issues.

(Branch secretary)

It is difficult because you can only do so much and since incorporation we've had so many battles and things slide. We did have a Women's Committee but it faded away . . . we're going to try and get that going again.

(Branch chair)

The whole climate has changed, not just not being under ILEA but in NATFHE as well. There's been a decline in the number of women's committees that exist and race initiatives as well and that's because higher education has been in such turmoil over the last few years. Equal opportunities is not at the top of anyone's agenda any more and however much you disagree with that it's how it is. It's been ground away. There has never been a greater need for self-organization among women and black people, but there isn't that push. You can't do it unless people are willing to take it on.

(NATFHE activist)

Staff are worried about their jobs. Higher education is such a pressurized sector now. League tables, short-term contracts, the research ratings exercise. So equal opportunities has slipped down the list, it's been a casualty if you like, but I don't think that's just in higher education, it's in other institutions too.

(Branch treasurer)

There are a number of interesting themes that can be identified in these responses. Perhaps the one that emerges most clearly is the 'changing times' theme. It is this argument that underpins all the accounts as to why this branch of NATFHE had so low a profile on equal opportunities, even though the branch officials were broadly sympathetic to the discourse. Incorporation, the abolition of ILEA, managerialism, concern over ratings and institutional prestige and the changes in higher education are all elements in the 'changing times' syndrome, as is the evocation of external factors – that is, the retreat from local authority equality initiatives of the 1980s, the end of what Gilroy (1990) has termed 'radicalism in the rates', and its replacement with what Myers (1990: 295) has identified as a climate of 'equiphobia'. While correctly highlighting the influence of such factors, NATFHE officials at Castlebrook University had not been active in challenging the slippage sustained by equal opportunities issues in relation to the university. NATHFE in this case study had, in effect, allowed the relegation of equal opportunities to the peripheries of the institution's concerns while, somewhat ironically, recognizing that this process was occurring.

Wider perceptions of the local AUT and NATFHE relationship to equal opportunities

Equal opportunities activists/officials

How did those university staff members who were involved with equal opportunities work in the case-study universities perceive the responses of the AUT and NATFHE to equality issues? Given the inactive position that these unions had taken up locally, it was not particularly surprising, although still significant, that the overwhelming majority of respondents in this category had little or no contact with the AUT and NATFHE in terms of equal opportunities. Even at Castlebrook University, where the branch officials presented themselves as supportive of an equal opportunities agenda, none of those respondents with formal or informal involvement with equal opportunities had used the NATFHE branch as a forum for equality struggles. For example, the only academic staff representative on the university's central Equal Opportunities Committee stated that:

> *I've never thought about NATFHE in relation to equal opportunities at all . . .*
> I know there are one or two committed women in NATFHE here, but on the whole I think it's a bastion of the traditional left which has only ever paid lip service to race and gender. From what I've seen, NATFHE here hasn't contributed to any equal opportunities debates and if it did it would be in a conflict situation with management, which is the traditional position of unions, and it wouldn't be able to work with management and that's the trouble with things like equal opportunities, there has to be a degree of cooperation (emphasis added).

This response is interesting not only because NATFHE is not considered in relation to equal opportunities issues, but also because of the perception of its traditional leftism as being at odds with race and gender interests. In other words, even where a union branch is considered to be political, it is perceived to be a form of politicization that cannot accommodate the 'new' politics associated with an equality agenda.

At Northfield University, NATFHE officials were associated with equal opportunities but only in very negative terms. The hostility of the NATFHE branch towards equal opportunities was publicly known within the university. For example, a senior lecturer in social policy and a former member of the university's Racial Equality Centre explained:

> *SL*: I've been very disappointed with NATFHE, especially here. NATFHE operates here in the worst kind of trade union model where there's a narrow clique of activists who've been there for years and whose main activity is trying to stop other people from becoming union activists. In my experience, there's never been any union support, never mind initiation, for equality initiatives. It would be more accurate to say they've been opposed to them, especially the Race Equality Unit. Rumour is

that NATFHE actually tried to block the unit being set up and stop it having anything to do with staff recruitment or development or training . . . whether the rumour was true or not is irrelevant because people certainly believed that NATFHE was opposed to it [the Racial Equality Unit]. I always felt resistance from NATFHE . . . sometimes you couldn't quite put your finger on it, but it was there, particularly towards the black members of the unit . . . I don't think the white workers had the same kind of response.

SN: But do you think that NATFHE has a responsibility or role in equal opportunities and equality issues?

SL: Oh it should have, definitely, but I can't be bothered with taking that up. I'm quite bitter about NATFHE and I'm only a member be-cause I believe in supporting trade unions, even when they treat me like they have.

This response highlights a number of important issues: the *active* opposi-tion of union officials to equality initiatives, particularly in relation to race; the ways in which this active opposition permeates the wider institution and thereby undermines both the initiative and the individuals involved in implementing the initiative; and the ways in which a local union branch can be dominated by a 'narrow clique', which is able to control/dictate the union's agenda and effectively inhibit wider participation in the union. This reflects the Marxist and neo-Marxist critiques of the trade union move-ment, which have focused on the ways in which the conservatism of trade union officials dominate the political character of trade unions (J. Kelly, 1988; see Chapter 3). At Northfield University, the conservatism of NATFHE officials and their public opposition to equality policies served to lower dra-matically any *expectation* of union support for those policies. For example, although the Women's Unit coordinator at Northfield University felt that 'ideally' NATFHE should be involved with the university's equal opportun-ities policies, such support had never occurred in practice:

WUC: I think NATFHE could do a lot more . . . they could be more pro-active and promote issues, but I don't tend to really associate NATFHE with equal opportunities here. There's no history of union support and they have no relationship with the Women's Unit and I know they haven't been happy with our harassment codes and the language guide.

SN: Would you like the Women's Unit to liaise more with the union?

WUC: I suppose we could do something about trying to do that but . . . they've never approached us and, like I say, I don't know how supportive they would actually be. The union wouldn't be the first place I'd go for backing, *but I haven't really ever considered it that much* (emphasis added).

There were, then, three recurring themes in the ways in which formal and informal equal opportunities activists perceived the AUT and NATFHE in relation to equal opportunities concerns. The first of these themes was indifference to the AUT and NATFHE and little consideration of the unions in terms of equal opportunities activity. The second theme was that the AUT and NATFHE could or should have a role in relation to equal opportunities, but there was little expectation of such a role being taken up. The third theme was anger towards the academic unions because of unmet expectations and the active anti-equal opportunities position of some local associations. A fourth theme that occurred less often, and mainly in relation to the AUT, was indifference to, or low expectations of, the local association but an acknowledgement that national AUT equal opportunities policy documents and the triennial *AUT Woman* had been useful at some stage of the respondents' own equal opportunities work. For example, the equal opportunities officer at Russell College told me that:

> I've never really campaigned with the AUT in the university ... they've never opposed anything as far as I know and I do expect them to be supportive but this association doesn't have a high profile. I think they've mainly been active on pay and contracts and things ... but I have used some of their national policy statements and I always read the *AUT Woman* bulletin ... that's quite good.

Similarly, at Peoples University, the Director of the Equal Opportunities Unit felt that: 'Some of the policy documents that come from AUT headquarters have been useful ... so no, the association here isn't involved in equal opportunities, but the AUT more generally has been concerned I think'.

This fourth response is particularly interesting because it emphasizes the passivity and inactivity of the local trade unions, while, at the same time, it provides a glimpse into the *potential* alliance between the unions and those responsible or involved with equality issues in higher education.

Senior management

Senior management approaches towards the AUT and NATFHE were important for a number of reasons, not least because members of senior management tended to be union members. The willingness of senior management to join academic trade unions has to be seen as a reflection of the political character of those unions as well as a factor that potentially tempers that political character.

There was a certain predictability in the majority of responses from senior management in relation to questions about the role and responsibility of the AUT and/or NATFHE – that is, that the priorities of these unions should be confined to representing membership interests in traditional areas of trade union concern. If there was a role for the AUT and NATFHE in equal opportunities policies processes, then this was secondary to its primary task and should be a supportive and cooperative, rather than an initiating or campaigning, role. For example, the director of Russell College explained:

> The job of the AUT, as with all unions, is or should be to represent the interests of their members, *their job isn't to cure the world*. The interests of the members is that there should be proper treatment . . . *employment issues* must be at the forefront of any union. The AUT can lend higher education a role in equal opportunities but it can't be their primary role to say we want our members to work in institutions which have a particular kind of ethos, although that is important . . . but they are not an academic body, they are a body serving the interests of their members and once people get too far away from that, have a fine policy or something, then they get a drift away in numbers. They have to be fairly close to their members wishes (emphasis added).

Despite the predictability of this statement, this does not detract from its more fascinating theme: that once a union strays away from traditional union areas ('employment issues') into more overtly political (equality) issues ('curing the world'), then this is against the best interests of its membership and this will be reflected in a decline in membership. What is particularly significant here is not simply that the director of Russell College believes that trade unions should confine themselves to traditional (de-politicized/a-political)[2] issues in higher education, but also that equal opportunities, although not actually referred to directly, represents only a minority (politically motivated) interest, which is both alien to, and will alienate, the majority of members. The following excerpts from interview transcripts with senior managers all reflect one or more of the central aspects of these views:

> NATFHE, like any union, is there to represent the best interests of *all* its members, that's its job . . . to *sensibly* negotiate on behalf of those members.
> (Pro-vice-chancellor, Castlebrook University, emphasis added)

> I expect NATFHE to be *supportive* of our equal opportunities initiatives and codes of practice. They don't actually have that much involvement with equal opportunities here but that's my expectation in terms of their role, although I suppose I see pay and conditions of service, staff development as more within NATFHE's usual area.
> (Head of personnel services, Castlebrook University,
> emphasis added)

> *Backing* is the word that comes to mind in relation to the AUT and equal opportunities in the university. Maybe they should initiate a bit more because that's always good . . . but definitely backing for the policies.
> (Pro-vice-chancellor, Peoples University, emphasis added)

What emerges from these excerpts is the notion that union responsibility focuses on, and takes place according to, a narrow set of prescribed areas – pay, conditions of service, etc. While there are expectations of the AUT and NATFHE in terms of equal opportunities, these are confined to a 'supportive', 'backing' and essentially passive role. That senior management did not expect the AUT and NATFHE to take a particularly proactive position in relation to equality issues was reflected in these unions lack of formal representation (with the exception of Russell College) in the case study universities' equal opportunities structures. Questioning whether it was actually desirable to have formal union representation on universities' equal opportunities structures, senior management respondents either pointed to the existence of Joint Union Negotiating Committees or to the fact that at least one member of staff involved in the institutions' equal opportunities structure would also be an AUT or NATFHE member and so, while not being formally represented, there would, indirectly, be AUT or NATFHE members who were involved in the policy processes:

> We have the Joint Union Negotiating Committee and that's the main place where the university talks to the unions on campus... that's where the unions bring up the issues with which they're concerned.
> (Pro-vice-chancellor, Peoples University)

> No, we don't have specific places for union representatives on the Equal Opportunities Committee but inevitably a number of the members of that committee will also be NATFHE members, so the union is represented in that way. They may be wearing a different hat but the union is there.
> (Deputy director, Northfield University)

It was only in Northfield University that there was any significant deviation from the 'the AUT/NATFHE should be supportive of equal opportunities but they have other things to do' position. When I interviewed the director, he was unambiguously critical of NATFHE, stating that:

> All trade unions must have an interest in the pursuit of equal opportunities policies. I think you might expect NATFHE, because of the sphere in which its members work, to be interested in equal opportunities, but the trade unions have been rather negative in terms of the pursuit of equal opportunities... I think it would not be unfair to say that I cannot think of an initiative that has come from NATFHE and I find it difficult to recall any positive support from NATFHE. I can only think of occasions when they have negatively attacked policies and procedures. I would describe NATFHE as at best passive, and at worst anti-equal opportunities.

Although it presents a departure from the more common position taken by senior management, this response has to be seen in terms of NATFHE's open hostility to equality issues and the university's heavily top-down model

of equal opportunities at Northfield (see Chapter 5). There is also a particular irony in a senior management figure suggesting that a trade union
adopt a more radical political position within the university. This under-
lines the complexities and contradictions that an equal opportunities agenda
can produce in institutions.

Conclusion

This chapter has argued that neither the AUT or NATFHE played a supportive or initiating role in relation to equal opportunities in the four case-
study universities. Inactivity characterized the response of the local union
associations studied. However, the very *inactivity* of the local AUT and
NATFHE organizations in relation to equal opportunities issues has to be
understood as actually representing a form of *activity*. In other words, the
four associations had not simply not responded to equality policies, rather
they had chosen to respond in an inactive way. This common inactivity was
differentiated by a number of factors in each case study: apathy and weak
organization (Russell College); hostility towards and suspicion of equal
opportunities (Peoples University, Northfield University); and exclusion and
the slippage of equal opportunities issues as a priority area on the union
agenda (Castlebrook University). The differing positions that the AUT and
NATFHE had taken up locally in relation to equality questions and their
shared inactivity had created a situation in which those members of staff
who were involved with equal opportunities policy processes in the case-
study universities, did not perceive these unions as sites of support for equal
opportunities or associate the AUT and NATFHE as forums in which issues
of social justice could be raised and campaigned on. Senior management
tended to view the role of the AUT and NATFHE in relation to equal
opportunities as one which should be passively supportive rather than pro-
active and initiating.

There was a significant policy–practice gap between the equal opportunities policies which the AUT and NATFHE had developed at a national
level and their uptake at a local level. Reflecting the 'post equal opportunities' era of the 1990s, there was some evidence that at the national level
of both the AUT and NATFHE there had been a drift away from a concern
with equality issues rather than a reassessment or realignment of equal
opportunities and anti-racist strategies. Examples of this drift include the
dated nature of both the AUT and NATFHE's equality policy documents;
NATFHE's re-naming of its Anti-Racist Committee to the Racial Equality
Committee; the uncertain future of the AUT's Equal Opportunities Committee and the rarity of its meetings. Against this background, NATFHE's
appointment of a part-time national equal opportunities officer appears
as a tokenistic, tired and tried, old-style initiative rather than a committed
new approach at the cutting edge of contemporary strategies around equality
concerns.

The AUT and NATFHE have not played a central role in the response of the higher education sector to issues of equal opportunities. The initiatives that both unions have developed at a national level have tended to operate as symbolic gestures and have not influenced the activities of local union associations. Consequently, local associations have chosen either not to respond to, or be involved with, universities' equal opportunities agendas, and have raised questions as to whether equal opportunities actually represents an area in which trade unions should or can have a particular responsibility.

7

Conclusions

Introduction

This concluding chapter seeks to draw together the key themes of the arguments made throughout the preceding chapters. However, it is also my intention here not only to look back but also to look forward. Whenever I have publicly presented my arguments and fieldwork findings (at conferences, in seminars, to colleagues), there has tended to be a common response on the part of these occasional audiences. This response can be summarized by two related questions: 'What can we do to address the issues of inequality?' and 'How can we make equal opportunities policies and anti-racist initiatives work?'

In many ways, such questions, and potential answers, are pragmatically orientated and understandably, so. Consequently, one aspect of 'looking forward' will be concerned with identifying and suggesting ways in which equal opportunities policies, their formation and their implementation, can be more effectively harnessed to genuine attempts to address issues of (in)equality and social justice. Yet there is a need to recognize the limits of pragmatism and pragmatically orientated questions. As Goldberg (1993: 215) argues, the notion of pragmatism 'is taken by many to carry connotations of an unprincipled instrumentalism, a technological tampering that services power and control'. Similarly, my ambivalence with regard to providing pragmatic solutions or recommendations is rooted in the critique that I have sought to offer of the equal opportunities discourse throughout this book. In other words, to become bound up in searching for practical (possible) solutions can circumvent the more fundamental questions that exist around the ability of the equal opportunities discourse itself (and the type of strategies that conventionally emerge from it) to make a meaningful difference to equality issues. Some caution, then, is needed when answering the question 'what is to be done?' in purely pragmatist terms.

Looking back

The themes of contradiction and ambiguity lie at the heart of my explorations of higher education's responses to equal opportunities questions. These themes have consistently emerged in differing but connected ways: the methodological contradictions encountered in the research process itself; the political contradictions which the research sites encompassed; the ambiguous findings of the research. The methodological discussions in Chapter 1 were dominated by the tensions which arose through my attempts to employ both anti-racist (i.e. challenging) and traditional feminist (i.e. reciprocal, egalitarian) approaches to researching equality questions in a research site primarily made up of powerful professional respondents. While my unresolved negotiations of these contradictions (the confrontational feminist researcher) were significant in themselves, they also highlighted broader difficulties with the concept of anti-racism (oppositional and politicized) and the subsequent caution with which it is approached by organizations in terms of policy initiatives regarding race and equality. As research sites, higher education and (academic) trade unions are particularly fascinating. Both have been 'sympathetically' associated with issues of social justice and equal opportunities. However, both can be identified as organizations in which traditionalism and hierarchy (higher education) and conservatism and defensiveness (academic trade unions) have played key roles (Chapters 2 and 3). Within such contexts, the responses of higher education and academic trade unions to the arrival of equal opportunities onto their agendas has been ambiguous. This ambiguity has a duality to it, both in the nature of the types of responses made and in equal opportunities policies themselves. I have argued that the terms 'equal opportunities' and 'anti-racism' have contested meanings and that equality initiatives are often fragile and tend to become 'arenas of struggle' as the municipal experience of the 1980s illustrated. Correspondingly, the research findings from the four case-study universities and the AUT and NATFHE unions within these were characterized by contradiction and tension. For the case-study universities, equal opportunities was an area that each institution had addressed in terms of the development of policy documents and the establishment of various forms of equality structures to implement and generate policy. Yet, in the everyday, micro world of the universities, equality initiatives were subjected to narrow, managerial ownership, marginalization and fragmentation. Within this world, there was an absence of consensus in terms of what equal opportunities actually meant and what the aims of equal opportunities policies actually were on the part of senior management, equal opportunities officials and those informally involved with equal opportunities. As Farish *et al.* (1995: 185) note:

> Genuine equality of opportunity for staff (and students) often appears to be a combination of chimera and the holy grail: *unimaginable* because there are so many different views of what it might consist of, and

unattainable because of widely differing opinions about how it might be achieved (original emphasis).

Because genuine equality of opportunity can be and has been seen as unimaginable, unattainable (and *undesirable*), a process of depoliticization can then accompany equality discourses and policies. The depoliticization of equality issues is an organizational attempt to maximize consent and minimize dissent. In other words, reducing the political content of equal opportunities makes equality discourses and policies more acceptable and less contested. Such a depoliticization process was evident in the responses that the case-study universities had made towards equal opportunities. In other words, the acceptability of equality discourses and policies in the case-study universities relied on their ability to be depoliticized and collapsed into a fairness/removal of barriers interpretation. Accompanying this was an overwhelming tendency within the case-study universities to adopt a technicist and rationalist based policy approach to equality issues seen, for example, in the similarity of the areas covered in the equal opportunities policy documents and in the common establishment of such structures as equal opportunities committees, advisory committees and specialist posts. However, in the everyday, micro world of the case-study universities, questions of equal opportunities, particularly those around race, tended to seep continually out of this depoliticization process. Consequently, equal opportunities policies remained contested and the technicist strategies put in place to implement them were often rendered ineffective and marginal (Chapter 5).

Ambiguity and contradiction characterized the positions which the AUT and NATFHE had taken up in relation to equal opportunities questions. On the one hand, at a national level, both unions had developed equal opportunities policy texts and internal equal opportunities structures. Yet on the other hand, at a local level, such initiatives had had little impact. Within all four case-study universities, the AUT and NATFHE had chosen to respond inactively to the universities' equal opportunities programmes, although the contexts for this inactivity varied in each case study: apathy (Russell College), hostility and suspicion (Peoples University, Northfield University) and exclusion (Castlebrook University). Particularly significant were the doubts expressed by local AUT and NATFHE officials as to whether equal opportunities issues were an area in which trade unions should be naturally involved (Chapter 6). Given the degree of inactivity (and hostility) on the part of academic trade unions towards equal opportunities issues, it is not particularly surprising that those respondents formally and informally involved in equal opportunities work in each university tended not to perceive the AUT and NATFHE as sympathetic allies.

Linked to the themes of ambiguity and contradiction, the problematic status of race within equality discourses and policies has been central to the book. The area of race was one which (white) respondents openly acknowledged feeling uncomfortable and uncertain discussing (Chapter 1). Higher education's shift from elitism to expansionism and the corresponding debates as to declining academic standards and 'mickey mouse' (i.e. new) universities are debates which contain a racialized sub-text which relates more black and other minority ethnic students entering the higher education system with less academic excellence (Chapter 2). As higher education has demonstrated racist tendencies – the exclusion of black student applicants (CRE, 1988) and the production of racialized academic knowledge, which has been of use to the state (Goldberg, 1993) – so too has the trade union movement. Although the trade union movement has attempted to address the issues of racial inequality and relocate itself from its early 'colour-blind' position, this relocation has tended to be largely symbolic. That race is a specifically contentious area for organizations (and individuals) was also illustrated in the ways in which the racial equality and anti-racist initiatives of local authorities were particularly singled out for attack by the media and the New Right during the 1980s (Gordon, 1990).

The problematic status of race within equality discourses and policy-making was reflected in the fieldwork findings. This was manifested in a number of ways: *silence* in the case studies' equal opportunities texts on the issue of anti-racism; an openly confessed *fear* and inability to 'talk race' (hooks, 1996) on the part of (white) respondents; the *collapse* of racial equality questions into the areas of access and monitoring; the marginalization of specific structures put in place to work on racial equality (seen in particular in Northfield University); and *inactivity* on the part of local academic trade unions in response to racial equality questions. I have argued that the entry of equal opportunities issues onto the higher education agenda has been conditional on a process of depoliticization of those issues. In this way, gender and (increasingly) disability were areas which received policy attention because they can be collapsed into such technicist categories as childcare, maternity provision and wheelchair access. Sexuality had a very minimalist and doubtful place in equal opportunities work. While race is an area that has an unchallenged place within equality discourse and policy-making, the difficulties in depoliticizing race meant that it had been marginalized and presented a particularly contested profile. Divorcing equal opportunities from the broader context of social justice and the complex, multidimensional relations of power and oppression, has limited the effectiveness of *all* equality initiatives but has impacted more fundamentally on race initiatives. Against this background, it is not surprising that the more recent criticisms that have been levelled at the concept of anti-racism and anti-racist strategies by some commentators on the left (Macdonald *et al.*, 1989; Gilroy, 1990; Modood, 1992) have not received attention within higher education or academic trade unions. Progressive criticisms of equality discourses and policies (see also Cockburn, 1992) that highlight the complexities of racialized relations and the multidimensional nature of racial (and gendered) oppression and advocate non-essentialist counter-responses have a difficulty in being heard in such bureaucratic organizations as higher education institutions and trade unions. This difficulty exists not only because of the reluctance of organizational elites and policy-makers to take on board the political dimensions of equal opportunities, but also because the technicist and rationalist approaches which characterize the current responses to equality issues do not allow space for such alternative formations of equality policy generation and implementation. As I noted earlier, there is a need to move equal opportunities policies away from the technicist strategic forms they commonly take. In the Preface, I cited the findings from the 1994 Students Union Survey into racial and sexual harassment at Oxford University. While what this survey revealed was very disturbing, as significant was the failure of the Harassment Advisory Panel, (established by the university after a similar survey conducted in 1990 had also revealed high levels of sexual and racial harassment), to have any positive impact on harassment within the institution. The 1994 survey found that the vast majority of students questioned had no knowledge of the existence of the Panel (*The Times*, 8 November 1994).

Is it possible to move beyond the inadequacies of technicist equal opportunities structures and is it possible to force a limited and constrained discourse (as equal opportunities is) to address equality issues in a more meaningful way?

Looking forward

New approaches to equality policies

The issue here is not whether higher education has responded to equal opportunities concerns or not – equal opportunities discourses and policies have secured a place on individual university agendas (and the agendas of the two main academic trade unions) (CUCO, 1994). The issue here is the nature of the responses that have been made. While the *Equal Opportunities Review* (1995: 30) optimistically argues that 'there are *encouraging* signs of a changing climate within the universities' (emphasis added), my own research reveals a more complex and disputed response to equal opportunities issues (see also Heward and Taylor, 1993; Farish *et al.*, 1995). Within higher education and the AUT and NATFHE, there is often a nebulous relationship between equal opportunities and issues of social justice. This relationship has to be dismantled and equal opportunities discourses and policies have to be rebuilt in such a way that they occupy a central place, as a real concern, in the everyday world of universities.

Among the key findings of the fieldwork research in the case studies were: (1) the narrow (mainly managerial) ownership of the equality policies; (2) the marginalization (isolation) of equality structures and the marginalization (reduction) of equality issues to such areas as access, non-discrimination, monitoring and fair interviewing; (3) the development of a fragmented depoliticized hierarchy within the equal opportunities rubric; and (4) the inactivity and suspicion on the part of local academic trade unions.

Addressing these areas could lead to a significant shift in the effectiveness of equal opportunities policies.

Some recommendations for change

The managerial control or top-down model of equal opportunities that prevailed in the case studies needs to be reviewed and replaced with a process involving a much higher degree of concerted, open and widespread consultation and debate throughout the institutions. This needs to be combined with a centralized but democratic process of on-going policy generation. The benefits in terms of having a wider consultative basis for policy generation would be reflected in the wider ownership of, and thereby commitment to, equality policies. Having a broader base of policy ownership would serve to increase both awareness/knowledge of the policies and strengthen their support within the institutions. While it is vital to retain management approval as far as possible for equality work, a far less intimidating management style, with less masculine modes of operating than was in evidence in the four case studies, would enable a growth of involvement, and more positive policy receivership, within the institutions.

Linked to this is the need for more careful 'public relations' work for all equality-related initiatives. More detailed explanations of the rationale for such initiatives is required. Such contextualization also needs to be coupled with the provision of guidelines on how to implement the initiatives. In order to increase approval for equality policies on the ground. While such measures may slow policy processes down, but this very slowness may be more effective in widening the ownership of equal opportunities policies while at the same time it would allow a space for a more reflexive, evaluatory and self-critical approach in terms of what equality questions need to be addressed and how. Accompanying such changes is the need to see equal opportunities policy processes as never-ending (Farish *et al.*, 1995). There was a tendency in the four universities and the AUT and NATFHE to view the policy process as static. In other words, once a policy had been formulated and procedures put in place to implement that policy, then that is as far as the process goes. The relative absence of evaluatory documents or exercises was a clear reflection of this. Equality policies cannot be viewed as complete, but instead need to be subject to continual, self-critical processes of review.

The marginalization of the specific structures established to formulate and especially implement equality policies was a process which had a profound and adverse affect on equal opportunities policies and their perceived status within the institutions. This was most pronounced in Northfield University, where the race-related initiatives had been particularly sidelined. These initiatives had failed to impact in a productive or effective way on the ethos or culture of the university. Rather, the Race Equality Unit had been relegated to 'special needs', community liaison and support work within the broader remit of the Access Unit. The individual equal opportunities posts within the university's faculties were stigmatized, isolated and treated with hostility or suspicion. Despite attempts to raise the issues of race within the institution, they were not grounded within an anti-racist context or an institutional ethos of anti-racism. Rather, they appeared to float, disembodied from the main body of the university. Similarly, at Russell College, the department-wide system of equal opportunities consultants was largely ineffective, the position often reluctantly taken on by a staff member and characterized by a lack of activity and a widespread perception among the consultants that, if there were no equal opportunities related complaints being made, then there were no problems in the area. While a training or induction period for staff whose brief covers equality issues would prove a beneficial measure, given the wider (institutional) lack of commitment to equality concerns, this would offer only a partial solution.

A more effective solution could be to ensure a 'coherent policy structure in which different policies and initiatives are systematically integrated' (Farish *et al.*, 1995: 178). For example, at Northfield, the university which had pursued the most overtly separatist strategy in relation to equal opportunities, the absence of combined work between the Women's Unit and the Racial Equality Centre was particularly striking. In the remaining case-study universities, which had adopted more integrationist approaches – for example, an Equal Opportunities Unit at Peoples University, an equal opportunities officer at Russell College and the Equal Opportunities Committees at Castlebrook University – there was an equally urgent need for a policy structure that united areas with different priorities and avoided promoting homogeneous solutions for all issues. In other words, there needs to be a combination of, or balance between, separatist and integrationist policy approaches to equal opportunities issues. This would have an impact on the tendency for the different areas of equal opportunities to develop into fragmented and competing hierarchies. Such hierarchies could also be avoided if institutions (universities and trade unions) were more willing to recognize historical patterns of disadvantage and the inherently political nature of these patterns. Reducing race into issues of access, monitoring and multicultural curriculum will not challenge racism, in the same way that relegating gender to flexi-time, job-share and childcare provision won't challenge sexism. Similarly, 'fair interviewing' will not, in itself, fundamentally alter the recruitment or employment of women and black and other minority ethnic staff. Rather, such approaches marginalize the bigger questions which higher education needs to ask itself regarding black and minority ethnic and women staff and students, and racist and sexist attitudes and/ or practices. Technicist and rationalist approaches to equal opportunities issues are severely limited in their ability to effect fundamental change. Although these do not necessarily have to be abandoned, their limitations must be recognized and the experiences of previously excluded groups in the everyday world of the institution have to be incorporated into policy-making processes.

The absence of any reference to anti-racism in the policy texts, the absence of anti-racist policy initiatives and the confusion and 'fear' on the part of white respondents that seemed to arise whenever the subject of race and racism was brought up in my interviews, all contribute to a picture of higher education in which, in contrast to compulsory or pre-sixteen education, the old dichotomous debates between multicultural and anti-racist education have never taken place. That these older debates have not occurred within higher education contextualizes the significant absence of any of the more recent debates that anti-racism has engendered (Macdonald *et al.*, 1989; Gilroy, 1990; Rattansi, 1992). While higher education may have evaded these debates, the concept of anti-racism (and related strategies) must find itself a secure and unassailable place on higher education's long-term agenda. However, higher education does not approach anti-racism with, as it were, a blank page. Higher education has not ignored race: as I have argued in Chapter 6, higher education has attempted to manage race by placing it in depoliticized categories and has clearly engaged in deracialized discourses. Yet, if there were to be a commitment to anti-racism, higher education would be able to draw on municipal, pre-sixteen and further education experiences and avoid some of the damaging pitfalls that previous anti-racist policies and initiatives have fallen into – that is, the black/white dichotomy, whereby 'racism is placed in some kind of moral vacuum and is totally divorced from the more complex reality of human relations' (Macdonald *et al.*, 1989: 402).

Anti-racism has still to find its way onto the agenda of higher education. Equal opportunities, which has obtained a place on that agenda, must be revitalized and allowed out of the confined and limited arenas in which it has been permitted to operate. Both within higher education institutions and academic trade unions, there is an urgent need for equal opportunities to be harnessed to genuine concerns surrounding the issues of equity and social justice, through the establishment of an ethos or culture which promotes equality and anti-oppressive and non-discriminatory attitudes and practices.

Conclusion

This final chapter has sought to reflect on the various themes of each of the preceding chapters. I have been concerned with three central arguments in this book. First, I have argued that equal opportunities discourses and the strategies that have most conventionally emerged from these are not adequate either to alleviate or challenge directly the issues of (in)equality (Chapters 4, 5 and 6). Second, I have argued that although the equal opportunities (if not an anti-racist) discourse has secured a place on higher education's agenda, the reasons for this acceptance rely on an ability to place equality questions within a depoliticized 'removal of barriers' interpretation of equal opportunities. The overwhelmingly technicist, standardized and rationalist strategies with which higher education institutions have attempted to approach equality issues have been ineffectual in terms of bringing about fundamental shifts in equality and in terms of minimizing the plethora of contested meanings attached to equal opportunities, and maximizing consent as to the need for, and aims of, equal opportunities policies (Chapters 4, 5 and 6). Third, I have argued that despite occupying a unique position in which to push equality issues forward in higher education, academic trade unions locally (and, to some extent, nationally) have taken at best a peripheral (apathetic) role, and at worst an adversarial (hostile) role, in relation to equal opportunities concerns (Chapters 3 and 6).

The second part of this concluding chapter has suggested that, despite these constraints and, in many ways, the bleakness of my research findings, some form of change in relation to equal opportunities within higher education and academic trade unions is possible. I have supported this by offering a number of pragmatically orientated ways forward for approaching equality issues within organizations. However, such changes rely on the recognition of the limitations of current ways of conceptualizing equal opportunities and related policy-making processes.

Appendix

Table A1 Breakdown of overall sample by gender and ethnicity

	Respondents					
Case studies	Total (n)	Total, males (n)	Total, females (n)	Black/ minority, males (n)	Black/ minority, females (n)	Total, black/ minority (n)
Universities	82	49	33	6	7	13
AUT and NATHFE	9	3	6	1	1	2
Total	91	52	39	7	8	15

Table A2 Breakdown by gender, ethnicity and respondent categories for each of the four case-study universities

			Gender		Ethnicity	
Institution	Respondent categories	Total (n)	Male (n)	Female (n)	Black/ minority (n)	White (n)
Peoples University	Senior management	6	5	1	—	6
	Formal equal opportunities officials	10	3	7	1	9
	Informal equal opportunities activists	3	2	1	2	1
	Local AUT officials	4	2	2	—	4

Table A2 (Cont'd)

			Gender		Ethnicity	
Institution	Respondent categories	Total (*n*)	Male (*n*)	Female (*n*)	Black/ minority (*n*)	White (*n*)
Russell	Senior management	4	4	—	—	4
College	Formal equal opportunities officials	8	2	6	—	8
	Informal equal opportunities activists	4	2	2	—	4
	Local AUT officials	4	3	1	—	4
Northfield	Senior management	4	4	—	—	4
University	Formal equal opportunities officials	9	4	5	6	3
	Informal equal opportunities activists	6	3	3	2	4
	Local NATFHE officials	3	3	—	—	3
Castlebrook	Senior management	8	8	—	—	8
University	Formal equal opportunities officials	2	1	1	—	2
	Informal equal opportunities activists	4	2	2	2	2
	Local NATFHE officials	3	1	2	—	3
Total interviews (*n*)		82	49	33	13	69

Table A3 Breakdown by gender and ethnicity for the two academic trade unions

		Gender		Ethnicity	
Union	Total (*n*)	Male (*n*)	Female (*n*)	Black/minority (*n*)	White (*n*)
AUT	4	1	3	—	4
NATFHE	5	2	3	2	3
Total	9	3	6	2	7

Table A4   Topics and questions covered in the interviews

I set out below the main themes and areas which I explored with my respondents. Being semi-structured interviews, the questions did not always run in the same order and, given that I was talking to different groups of respondents, various questions could, accordingly, be given more emphasis. However, I used exactly the same interview topics with each respondent.

- (Brief) life story and if or how respondent's brief relates to or incorporates equality-related work.
- Personal understanding of the term/concept of 'equal opportunities'.
- Personal understanding of the term/concept of 'anti-racism'.
- Impact of feminism in institution's equal opportunities debates.
- Does an equal opportunities ethos or culture exist in the university?
- Institution's equal opportunities structures: what are these, what are their histories, are they effective and what are their futures?
- Priority given to equal opportunities issues – resource allocation, monitoring programmes.
- Role of senior management in relation to equal opportunities policy formation and implementation.
- Where in the institution does the main pressure for equality activity and policies originate?
- Extent of ownership of equal opportunities policies.
- Have equal opportunities policies fragmented?
- What are the more 'comfortable' areas of equal opportunities debates and policy-making and what are the 'uncomfortable' or difficult areas and why?
- Personal priorities for equal opportunities agenda.
- University's priorities for equal opportunities agenda.
- Perceptions of AUT and/or NATFHE?
- Role and responsibilities of AUT and/or NATFHE in higher education institutions – priority areas for academic trade unions.
- Profile of AUT and NATFHE in equal opportunities debates and policy-making – high or low?
- Formal union representation within institution's equality structures.
- Do the AUT and NATFHE have a role and/or responsibility for equal opportunities issues?
- Can the AUT and/or NATFHE be characterized as being supportive and active in the area or hostile and inactive?
- How has the higher education sector as a whole responded to issues of equality and how has the changing climate of higher education impacted on the equal opportunities agenda?

Table A5 Case studies' equal opportunities policy documents

Universities
1. Castlebrook University
   Annual Report of Equal Opportunities Committee (1992–93)
   Enabling You, Students With Disabilities: A Guide to Policy and Procedure (1993)
   Equal Opportunities Policy Statement (1993)
   Making Equal Opportunities Work (1993)
   Racial, Sexual, Sexual Orientation and Disability Harassment Codes (1993)

2. Northfield University
   Equal Opportunities in Academic Affairs: A Policy Statement (1989)
   Equal Opportunities: A Declaration of Intent (1989)
   Equal Opportunities Committee: Annual Report (1992/3)
   Language and Equal Opportunities Guide (1992)
   Race Equality Unit Report (1990)
   Sexual and Racial Harassment Policy Statement (1990)
   Women's Progress: A Research Report (1988)
   Women's Unit Handbook (1993)

3. Peoples University
   Dealing with Sexual and Racial Harassment: A Code of Practice (1991)
   Equal Opportunities Action Plan (1990)
   Equal Opportunities: A Statement of Intent (1990)
   Equal Opportunities Guidelines for Course Material (1991)
   Equal Opportunities Unit Annual Reports (1992, 1994)
   Language and Image Guide (1992)
   Staff Newsletter (November 1992)
   University's Views on Equal Opportunities in Academic Affairs (1991)

4. Russell College
   Annual Report of University's Equal Opportunities Committee (1992/3)
   Equal Opportunities: A Policy Statement (1987)
   Minutes of Equal Opportunities Committee (1992/3)
   Report from University's Central Academic Board (1986)
   Sexual and Racial Harassment Code (1993)
   Terms of Reference for Equal Opportunities Consultants (1990)

Trade unions (some AUT and NATFHE publications are also included in the Bibliography)
1. AUT
   AUT Woman (issues published 1991–94)
   AUT Bulletin (issues published 1991–94)
   Ensuring Equal Opportunities for University Staff and Students from Ethnic Minorities (1987)
   Equal Opportunities: A Code of Practice for the Employment of Women (1984)
   Negotiating Pack for Positive Action (1995)
   Sexual Orientation and Employment in Universities (1990)
   Sexual Harassment: Code of Practice and Procedures for Individual Cases (1985)

Table A5 (Cont'd)

2. NATFHE
   Annual Report of Equal Opportunities Committee (1993–94)
   Breaking Down the Barriers (1981)
   Equal Opportunities Language Guide (1993)
   Equal Opportunities in Staff Appraisal and Development (1994)
   NATFHE Against Racism: A Resource Pack (1986)
   NATFHE Action Against Sexist or Racist Harassment: Branch Guidelines (1986)
   NATFHE Journal (issues published 1991–95)
   Sexual Orientation: An Equal Opportunities Discussion Paper (1986)
   Time for a New Initiative (1984)

Notes

Preface

1. While I use the term 'black' inclusively to refer to peoples of African, Caribbean and South Asian descent, it is not my intention to portray these groups as homogeneous or to deny difference and diversity. I use the term 'minority ethnic' to refer to groups which cannot be accommodated into the category 'black' but who are subject to racialized experiences.

Chapter 1   Researching Equal Opportunities in Higher Education: Issues, Dilemmas and Self

1. Although I use the term 'women' generically, 'this is not to say that all women are oppressed in the same ways, but rather to recognize that while oppression is common the forms it takes are conditioned precisely by race/ethnicity, age, sexuality and so forth' (Stanley, 1991: 207).

Chapter 2   The Changing Face of Higher Education in Britain

1. The percentage figures given for the size of black and minority ethnic communities in the university case-study localities are based on estimates given to me by respondents who knew the geographical area and who had formal responsibility for equal opportunities in each institution.
2. Under Section 11 of the 1966 Local Government Act, special funding was made available for local authorities, at the discretion of the Home Office, to support specific staff posts. These posts were to be established to meet the 'needs' of 'Commonwealth immigrants' (see Ben-Tovim *et al.*, 1992).
3. Since my research was conducted, this post has been renamed 'harassment officer' and has gone from being a full-time to a part-time post.

Chapter 3   Uneasy Relationships: Trade Unionism, Equal Opportunities and Academic Political Consciousness

1. In some ways, the 'fears' of the AUT leadership were realized in 1977 when the AUT engaged in a period of lengthy and unsuccessful negotiations over pay. These negotiations culminated in the high profile and militant 'Rectify the Anomaly' campaign, in which an estimated 7000 academic and academic-related

AUT members converged in a London demonstration, an event that the *Guardian* (17 November 1977) called a 'remarkable piece of industrial action'.
2. Significantly, until 1991 the Racial Equality Standing Committee had been called the Anti-Racist Advisory Committee. A senior NATFHE official explained that the committee had been renamed because 'Head Office considered the Anti-Racist Committee to be too *confrontational sounding*... I was in favour of keeping it the same, but that was the feeling at the top, that we wanted a *gentler approach*' (emphasis added).
3. The motion was not passed and I was told by a member of the NATFHE delegation how the AUT had decided to abstain from, and failed to second, the motion.

Chapter 4   Analysing Equal Opportunities Policy Documents

1. All the equality policy documents that were obtained from the four case-study universities and the AUT and NATFHE are listed in the Appendix.
2. That both the guide and the broader policy recommendations on equal opportunities and the curriculum had had limited impact on the production of course material was illustrated by an incident relayed to me by a sympathetic respondent. She told me that in a school board meeting of the education department (June, 1994), the dean of the school had produced a school development plan for 1995–2000 which made no reference to equal opportunities issues. Although when this was highlighted the dean had responded by stating that he would review the plan, the absence of any initial equal opportunities considerations would appear to indicate the marginality of the policy recommendations.
3. During the research there was a dispute in the sociology department as to the 9.00 a.m. timetabling of some of the courses. When students had raised the difficulties of this for those with home responsibilities, one course leader told me that she felt that the students were being unrealistic and expecting to be 'spoon-fed': 'I can understand that nine o'clock starts can be difficult for some students, but when they start working then that's the time when they'll be expected to arrive and we should be helping them get prepared for that... get used to that... everything can't always be done to suit students'.

Chapter 5   Equality Policies in the Everyday World of Universities

1. The disillusion expressed by the equal opportunities workers in terms of their role in the university was made more acute by the fact that they were all on short-term contracts.

Chapter 6   Academic Trade Union Responses to Equality Policies

1. The 1992–93 industrial dispute in Smethwick involving the GMB union and Asian workers also exposed the severe limitations of any 'new' or revised trade union approach to black workers (*Critical Eye*, Channel Four, November 1993).
2. This is not to argue that such areas are not political, but that it is the *treatment* of them that is a-political rather than the issue itself.

Bibliography

Abbassi, L. (1996) Equal opportunities and employment in higher education. Unpublished MA dissertation, Middlesex University.

Adams, H. (1983) Women's work in the interstices: Women in the academe, *Women's International Forum*, 6, 135–41.

Allen, S. (1982) Confusing categories and neglecting contradictions. In E. Cashmore and B. Troyna (eds), *Black Youth in Crisis*. London, Allen and Unwin.

Allen, S. and Bornat, J. (1970) Immigrants or workers. In S. Zubiada (ed.), *Race and Racialism*. London, Tavistock.

Allington, N. and O'Shaughnessy, N. (1992) *Light, Liberty and Learning: The Idea of a University Revisited*. Surrey, Education Unit.

Andersen, M. (1993) Studying across difference: Race, class and gender in qualitative research. In J. Stanfield and R. Dennis (eds), *Race and Ethnicity in Research Methods*. London, Sage.

Anderson, P. (1983) *In the Tracks of Historical Materialism*. London, Verso.

Anthias, F. and Yuval-Davis, N. (1992) *Racialised Boundaries: Race, Nation, Gender, Colour, Class and the Anti-racist Struggle*. London, Routledge.

Apple, M. (1977) Ivan Illich and deschooling society. In M. Young and G. Whitty (eds), *Society, State and Schooling*. Lewes, Falmer Press.

Ashton, D. (1982) *Youth in the Labour Market*, Research Paper No. 34. London, Department of Employment.

Atkinson, P. and Delamont, S. (1986) Bread and dreams or bread and circuses: A critique of case study research in education. In M. Shipman (ed.), *Educational Research*. Lewes, Falmer Press.

AUT (1988) *AUT Members Handbook*. London, AUT.

AUT (1989) *Rules of Association*. London, AUT.

AUT (1992) *Sex Discrimination in Universities: Report of an Academic Pay Audit Carried Out by the AUT Research Department*. London, AUT.

AUT (1993) *Update*. London, AUT.

Back, L. (1996) *New Ethnicities, Multiple Racisms*. London, University College London.

Back, L. and Solomos, J. (1992) Doing research, writing politics: The dilemmas of political intervention in research on racism. Paper presented to the *Workshop on the Politics of Racism*, Birkbeck College, University of London, April.

Bagilhole, B. (1994) Being different is a very difficult row to hoe: survival strategies of women academics. In S. Davies, C. Lubelska and J. Quinn (eds), *Changing the Subject: Women in Higher Education*. London, Taylor & Francis.

Bain, G. (1967) *Trade Union Growth and Recognition*, Research Paper No. 6, Royal Commission on Trade Unions and Employers Associations. London, HMSO.

Bain, G. (1972) *The Growth of White Collar Trade Unionism*. London, Heinemann.

Ball, C. (1990) *More Means Different: Widening Access to Higher Education*, Final Report Royal Society of Arts, London.

Ball, D. (1979) Self and identity in the context of deviance: The case of criminal abortion. In M. Wilson (ed.), *Social and Educational Research in Action*. Milton Keynes, Open University Press.

Ball, S. (1987) *The Micro-Politics of the School: Towards a Theory of School Organisation*. London, Methuen.

Ball, S. (1992) Ethnography in the corridors of power: The diary of a research tourist. Reflections on the fieldwork for politics and policy-making in education. Paper presented to an *ESRC Seminar on Methodological and Ethical Issues Associated with Research into the 1988 Education Reform Act*, University of Warwick, Coventry, March.

Ball, W. (1990) A critique of methods and ideologies in research on race and education. Paper presented to the *XIIth World Congress of Sociology*, Madrid, July–August.

Ball, W. (1991) The ethics and politics of doing anti-racist research in education: Key debates and dilemmas, *European Journal of Intercultural Studies*, 2, 35–49.

Ball, W. (1992) Critical social research, adult education and anti-racist feminist praxis, *Studies in the Education of Adults*, 24, 1–25.

Ball, W. (1994) Racial equality policies and the 'everyday world' of initial teacher training: The contribution of micro-politic and critical social research. Unpublished paper, University of Warwick.

Barker, M. (1981) *The New Racism: Conservatives and the Ideology of the Tribe*. London, Junction Books.

Beale, J. (1983) *Getting it Together: Women as Trade Unionists*. London, Pluto.

Becher, T. and Kogan, M. (1992) *Process and Structure in Higher Education*. London, Routledge.

Ben-Tovim, G., Gabriel, J., Law, I. and Stredder, K. (1986) *The Local Politics of Race*. London, Macmillan.

Ben-Tovim, G., Gabriel, J., Law, I. and Stredder, K. (1992) A political analysis of local struggles for racial equality. In P. Braham, A. Rattansi and R. Skellington (eds), *Racism and Antiracism: Inequalities, Opportunities and Policies*. London, Sage.

Benyon, J. and Solomos, J. (eds) (1987) *The Roots of Urban Unrest*. Oxford, Pergamon Press.

Berger, P. (1986) *The Capitalist Revolution: Fifty Propositions About Prosperity, Equality and Liberty*. New York, Basic Books.

Billingsley, A. (1970) Black families and white social science, *Journal of Social Issues*, 26(3), 127–42.

Bird, J. (1996) *Black Students and Higher Education: Rhetorics and Realities*. Buckingham, SRHE/Open University Press.

Blackburn, R. (1967) *Union Character and Social Class*. London, Batsford.

Blackman, I. and Perry, K. (1990) Skirting the issue: Lesbian fashion in the 1990s, *Feminist Review*, 34, 67–78.

Blackstone, T. and Fulton, O. (1974) Men and women academics: An Anglo-American comparison of subject choices and research activity, *Higher Education*, 3, 119–40.

Blackstone, T. and Fulton, O. (1975) Sex discrimination among university teachers – a British comparison, *British Journal of Sociology*, 26, 261–75.

Blase, J. (ed.) (1991) *The Politics of Life in Schools: Power, Conflict and Co-operation.* London, Sage.

Blyton, P., Ursell, G. and Nicholson, N. (1981) *The Dynamics of White Collar Unionism: A Study of Local Union Participation.* London, Academic Press.

Boddy, M. and Fudge, C. (eds) (1984) *Local Socialism.* London, Macmillan.

Bonnet, A. (1993) The formation of radical professional consciousness: The example of anti-racism, *Sociology*, 27(2), 281–97.

Bourne, J. with Sivanandan, A. (1980) Cheerleaders and ombudsmen: The sociology of race relations in Britain, *Race and Class*, XXI(4), 321–52.

Brah, A. (1993) 'Race' and 'culture' in the gendering of labour markets: South Asian young Muslim women and the labour market, *New Community*, 19(3), 441–58.

Brint, S. (1984) New class and cumulative trend explanations of the liberal political attitudes of professionals, *American Journal of Sociology*, 90, 30–71.

Brown, C. (1984) *Black and White Britain.* London, Heinemann.

Brown, C. and Gay, P. (1985) *Racial Discrimination: 17 Years After the Act.* London, Policy Studies Institute.

Bulmer, M. (ed.) (1984) *Sociological Research Methods.* London, Macmillan.

Bulmer, M. (1986) *Social Science and Social Policy.* London, Allen and Unwin.

Burgess, R. (1984) *In the Field: An Introduction to Fieldwork.* London, Allen and Unwin.

Burgess, T. and Pratt, J. (1974) *Polytechnics.* London, Pitman Press.

Burton, L. (1993) Management, 'race' and gender: An unlikely alliance?, *British Educational Research Journal*, 19(3), 275–90.

Cambridge, A.X. and Feuchtwang, S. (eds) (1990) *Anti-Racist Strategies.* Aldershot, Avebury.

Carby, H. (1982) White woman listen! Black feminism and the boundaries of sisterhood. In CCCS (ed.), *The Empire Strikes Back.* London, Hutchinson.

Carter, R. (1985) *Capitalism, Class Conflict and the New Middle Class.* London, Routledge and Kegan Paul.

Cashmore, E. and Troyna, B. (eds) (1982) *Black Youth in Crisis.* London, Allen and Unwin.

Chaucer, G. (1908) *The Prologue.* London, Everyman.

Cockburn, C. (1977) *The Local State: Management of Cities and People.* London, Pluto.

Cockburn, C. (1987) *Women, Trade Unions and Political Parties.* Fabian Research Series 349. London, Fabian Society.

Cockburn, C. (1992) *In the Way of Women: Men's Resistance to Sex Equality in Organisations.* Basingstoke, Macmillan.

Cohen, L. and Manion, L. (1980) *Research Methods in Education.* London, Croom Helm.

Commission for Racial Equality (1984) *Codes of Practice.* London, CRE.

Commission for Racial Equality (1985) *Review of the Race Relations Act 1976: Proposals for Change.* London, CRE.

Commission for Racial Equality (1986) *Black Teachers: The Challenge of Increasing the Supply.* Report of a residential seminar. London, CRE.

Commission for Racial Equality (1988) *Medical School Admissions: Report of Formal Investigation into St. George's Medical School.* London, CRE.

Commission for Racial Equality (1992) *Part of the Union: Trade Union Participation by Ethnic Minority Workers.* London, CRE.

Commission on University Career Opportunity (1994) *Report on Universities' Policies and Practices on Equal Opportunities in Employment.* London, CUCO.

Committee of Vice-Chancellors and Principals (1991) *Equal Opportunities in Employ-ment in Universities.* London, CVCP.

Connolly, P. (1993) Doing feminist and anti-racist research as a white male – a contradiction in terms? Paper presented to the *British Sociological Association Conference*, University of Essex, 5–8 April.

Coote, A. and Campbell, B. (1987) *Sweet Freedom: The Struggle for Women's Liberation.* London, Blackwell.

Cotgrove, S. and Duff, A. (1980) Environmentalism, middle class radicalism and politics, *Sociological Review*, 28, 333–51.

Craft, A. and Craft, M. (1983) The participation of ethnic minority pupils in further and higher education, *Education Research*, 25(1), 10–19.

Crompton, R. (1976) Approaches to the study of white collar trade unionism, *Sociology*, 10(3), 407–426.

Currie, D. and Kazi, H. (1987) Academic feminism and the process of de-radicalisation: Re-examining the issues, *Feminist Review*, 25, 74–98.

Dadzie, S., Bryan, B. and Scafe, S. (1986) *Heart of the Race: Black Women's Lives in Britain.* London, Virago.

Daniel, W. (1968) *Racial Disadvantage in England.* Harmondsworth, Penguin.

Dearlove, J. (1973) *The Politics of Policy in Local Government.* Cambridge, Cambridge University Press.

Delamont, S. (1978) The domestic ideology and women's education. In S. Delamont and L. Duffin (eds), *The Nineteenth Century Woman: Her Cultural and Physical World.* London, Croom Helm.

Donald, J. and Rattansi, A. (eds) (1992) *'Race', Culture and Difference.* London, Sage.

DuBois, B. (1983) Passionate scholarship: Notes on values, knowing and method in feminist social science. In G. Bowles and R. Duelli Klien (eds), *Theories of Women's Studies.* London, Routledge and Kegan Paul.

Duelli Klien, R. (1983) How to do what we want to do: Thoughts about feminist methodology. In G. Bowles and R. Duelli Klien (eds), *Theories of Women's Studies.* London, Routledge and Kegan Paul.

Dunleavy, P. (1980) *Urban Political Analysis.* London, Macmillan.

Dunleavy, P. (1984) The limits to local government. In M. Boddy and C. Fudge (eds), *Local Socialism.* London, Macmillan.

Edelman, M. (1964) *The Symbolic Uses of Politics.* Urbana, IL, University of Illinois Press.

Edelman, M. (1971) *Politics as Symbolic Action: Mass Arousal and Quiescence.* Chicago, IL, Markham.

Edelman, M. (1977) *Political Language: Words that Succeed and Policies that Fail.* New York, Academic Press.

Edelman, M. (1984) The political language of the helping professions. In M. Shapiro (ed.), *Language and Politics.* Oxford, Blackwell.

Edwards, J. (1987) *Positive Discrimination, Social Justice and Social Policy.* London, Tavistock.

Ehrenreich, B. and Ehrenreich, J. (1979) The professional-managerial class. In P. Walker (ed.), *Between Labour and Capital.* Hassocks, Sussex: Harvester Press.

Equal Opportunities Review (1995) No. 59, January, pp. 20–30.

Eyerman, R. (ed.) (1984) *Intellectuals, Universities and the State in Modern Western Societies.* Berkeley, CA, University of California Press.

Farish, M., McPake, J., Powney, J. and Weiner, G. (1995) *Equal Opportunities in Colleges and Universities: Towards Better Practices.* Buckingham, SRHE/Open University Press.

Farnham, D. (1991) Post-binarism and academic staff unions in the U.K., *Higher Education Review*, 24(1), 14–19.

Feuchtwang, S. (1990) The politics of equal opportunities in employment. In A.X. Cambridge and S. Feuchtwang (eds), *Anti-Racist Strategies*. Aldershot, Avebury.

Finch, J. (1984) It's great having someone to talk to: The ethics and politics of interviewing women. In C. Bell and H. Roberts (eds), *Social Researching: Politics, Problems and Practice*. London, Routledge and Kegan Paul.

Frankenberg, R. (1993) *White Women, Race Matters: The Social Construction of Whiteness*. London, Routledge.

Fryer, P. (1984) *Staying Power: The History of Black People in Britain*. London, Pluto.

Gallie, W.B. (1956) Essentially contested concepts. *Proceedings of the Aristotelian Society*, 56, 167–98.

Garabino, J. and Aussieker, B. (1975) *Faculty Bargaining: Change and Conflict*. New York, McGraw-Hill.

Garrard, J. (1971) *The English and Immigration 1880–1914*. Oxford, Oxford University Press.

Geiger, S. (1986) Women's life histories: Method and content, *Signs*, 11(6), 334–51.

Gelsthorpe, L. (1992) Response to Martyn Hammersley's paper 'on feminist methodology', *Sociology*, 26(2), 213–18.

Gerwirtz, S. and Ozga, J. (1993) Sex, lies and audiotape: Interviewing the education policy elite. Paper presented to the *Economic and Social Research Council 1988 Education Reform Act Research Seminar*, University of Warwick, Coventry, February.

Giles, G.J. (1977) The rise of the polytechnic in Britain. Paper presented to the international conference *Universities Today*, Dubrovnik.

Gillborn, D. (1995) *Race and Antiracism in Real Schools*. Buckingham, Open University Press.

Gilroy, P. (1980) Managing the 'underclass': A further note on the sociology of race relations in Britain. *Race and Class*, 22, 47–62.

Gilroy, P. (1987) *Ain't No Black in the Union Jack*. London, Hutchinson.

Gilroy, P. (1990) The end of anti-racism. In W. Ball and J. Solomos (eds), *Race and Local Politics*. London, Macmillan.

Gilroy, P. (1992) Foreword. In B. Hesse, D.K. Rai, C. Bennett and P. McGilchrist *Beneath the Surface: Racial Harassment*. Aldershot, Avebury.

Giroux, H. (1984) Ideology, agency and the process of schooling. In L. Barton and S. Walker (eds), *Social Crisis and Educational Research*. London, Croom Helm.

Goldberg, D.T. (1993) *Racist Culture: Philosophy and the Politics of Meaning*. Oxford, Blackwell.

Gordon, P. (1990) The dirty war: The new right and local authority anti-racism. In W. Ball and J. Solomos (eds), *Race and Local Politics*. London, Macmillan.

Gouldner, A. (1971) *The Coming Crisis in Western Sociology*. London, Heinemann.

Gouldner, A. (1979) *The Future of Intellectuals and the Rise of the New Class*. London, Macmillan.

Gramsci, A. (1919/1977) *Selections from Political Writings, 1910–1920* (selected and edited by Q. Hoare). London, Lawrence and Wishart.

Gramsci, A. (1921/1978) *Selections from Political Writings, 1921–1926* (selected and edited by Q. Hoare). London, Lawrence and Wishart.

Gramsci, A. (1971) On intellectuals. In Q. Hoare and G. Smith (eds), *Selections from the Prison Notebooks*. New York, International Publishers.

Greater London Council Anti-Racist Trade Union Working Group (1984) *Racism Within Trade Unions*. London, GLC.

Greater London Council (*c.* 1985) *Keep the GLC Working for London: Some Myths and Facts*. London, GLC.

Gundara, J. (1983) The social and political context: Education for a multicultural society. Paper presented to the *Geography and Education for a Multicultural Society Conference*, University of London, March.

Gutzmore, C. (1983) Capital, 'black youth' and crime, *Race and Class*, XXV(2), 13–30.

Habermas, J. (1972) *Knowledge and Human Interests*. London, Heinemann.

Hague, D. (1990) *Beyond Universities: A New Republic of the Intellect*. London, Institute of Economic Affairs.

Hall, S. (1992) New ethnicities. In J. Donald and A. Rattansi (eds), *'Race', Culture and Difference*. London, Sage.

Halsey, A. (1992) *The Decline of the Donnish Dominion*. London, Clarendon Press.

Halsey, A. and Trow, M. (1971) *The British Academics*. London, Faber and Faber.

Hammersley, M. (1992a) On feminist methodology, *Sociology*, 26(2), 187–206.

Hammersley, M. (1992b) *What's Wrong with Ethnography*. London, Routledge.

Hammersley, M. and Atkinson, P. (1995) *Ethnography: Principles in Practice*. London, Routledge.

Handy, C. and Aitken, R. (1986) *Understanding Schools as Organisations*. Harmondsworth, Penguin.

Hansard Society (1990) *Report of the Hansard Society Commission on Women at the Top*. London, Hansard Society.

Harding, S. (ed.) (1987) *Feminism and Methodology: Social Science Issues*. Milton Keynes, Open University Press.

Hargreaves, A. (1982) Resistance and relative autonomy theories: Problems of distortion and incoherence in recent Marxist analyses of education, *British Journal of Sociology of Education*, 3(2), 107–26.

Hargreaves, A. (1985) The micro–macro problem in the sociology of education. In R. Burgess (ed.), *Issues in Educational Research*. London, Falmer Press.

Harvey, L. (1990) *Critical Social Research*. London, Unwin Hyman.

Henry, M. (1994) Ivory towers and ebony women: The experiences of black women in higher education. In S. Davies, C. Lubelska and J. Quinn (eds), *Changing the Subject: Women in Higher Education*. London, Taylor and Francis.

Hesse, B., Rai, D., Bennett, C. and McGilchrist, P. (1992) *Beneath the Surface: Racial Harassment*. Aldershot, Avebury.

Heward, C. and Taylor, P. (1993) Effective and ineffective equal opportunities policies in higher education, *Critical Social Policy*, 37, 75–94.

Hickox, M. (1986) Has there been a British intelligentsia?, *British Journal of Sociology*, XXXVII(2), 221–40.

Hobsbawm, E. (1981) *The Forward March of Labour Halted?* London, Verso.

Honeyford, R. (1983) Multi-ethnic intolerance, *Salisbury Review*, 4, 12–13.

Honeyford, R. (1984) Education and race: An alternative view, *Salisbury Review*, 6, 30–2.

hooks, b. (1982) *Ain't I a Woman: Black Women and Feminism*. London, Pluto.

hooks, b. (1989) *Talking Back Thinking Feminist Thinking Black*. London, Sheba.

hooks, b. (1996) *Killing Rage, Ending Racism*. London, Penguin.

Hyman, R. (1971) *Marxism and the Sociology of Trade Unions*. London, Pluto.

Jenkins, R. and Solomos, J. (eds) (1989) *Racism and Equal Opportunities Policies in the 1980s*. Cambridge, Cambridge University Press.

Jewson, N. and Mason, D. (1986) Theory and practice of equal opportunities, *Sociological Review*, 34, 307–34.

Jewson, N., Mason, D., Waters, S. and Harvey, J. (1990) *Ethnic Minorities and Employment Practice: A Study of Six Organisations*. Research Paper No. 76. Leicester, Leicester University.

Jewson, N., Mason, D., Bowen, R., Mulvaney, K. and Parmar, S. (1991) Universities and ethnic minorities: The public face, *New Community*, 17, 183–99.

Jewson, N., Mason, D., Broadbent, J., Jenkins, S. and Thandi, H. (1993) *Polytechnics and Ethnic Minorities: The Public Face*. Discussion Paper. Leicester, Leicester University.

Joshi, S. and Carter, B. (1984) The role of Labour in the creation of a racist Britain, *Race and Class*, XXV(3), 53–70.

Keith, M. (1992) Angry writing: (Re)presenting the unethical world of the ethnographer, *Society and Space*, 10, 551–68.

Kelly, J. (1988) *Trade Unions and Socialist Politics*. London, Verso.

Kelly, L. (1988) *Surviving Sexual Violence*. London, Polity Press.

Kleingartner, A. and Hunt, E. (1986) *Academic Unionism in British Universities*. Berkeley, CA, Institute of Industrial Relations, University of California.

Knowles, C. (1992) *Race, Discourse and Labourism*. London, Routledge.

Kogan, M. and Kogan, D. (1983) *The Attack on Higher Education*. London, Kogan Page.

Labour Party (1985) *Positive Discrimination/Black People and the Labour Party*. London, Labour Party.

Lancashire Association of Trades Councils with Commission for Racial Equality (1985) *Trade Union Structures and Black Workers' Participation: A Study in Central Lancashire*. London, CRE.

Lansley, S., Goss, S. and Wolmar, C. (1989) *Councils in Conflict: The Rise and Fall of the Municipal Left*. Basingstoke, Macmillan.

Larson, M. (1979) *The Rise of Professionalism: A Sociological Analysis*. Berkeley, CA, University of California Press.

Larson, S. (1980) *Who Were the Fascists? Social Roots of European Fascism*. Oslo, Universitetsforlaget.

Lather, P. (1986) Research as praxis, *Harvard Educational Review*, 56(3), 257–77.

Law, I. (1996) *Racism, Ethnicity and Social Policy*. Hemel Hempstead, Prentice Hall.

Lawrence, E. (1981) White sociology, black struggle, *Multiracial Education*, 9(3), 3–17.

Lawrence, E. (1982) In the abundance of water the fool is thirsty: Sociology and black 'pathology'. In CCCS (ed.), *The Empire Strikes Back*. London, Hutchinson.

Lawrence, E. (1983) Book review, *Race and Class*, XXV(2), 95–9.

Lea, J. and Young, J. (1982) The riots in Britain in 1981: Urban violence and political marginalisation. In D. Cowell, T. Jones and J. Young (eds), *Policing the Riots*. London, Junction Books.

Lee, G. (1984) *Trade Unionism and Race*. A report to the West Midlands Regional Council of the Trades Union Congress.

Leicester, M. (1993) *Race for a Change in Continuing and Higher Education*. Buckingham, Open University Press.

Lenin, V. (1902/1988) *What is to be Done?* London, Penguin.

Leonard, P. and Malina, D. (1994) Caught between two worlds: Mothers as academics. In S. Davies, C. Lubelska and J. Quinn (eds), *Changing the Subject: Women in Higher Education*. London, Taylor and Francis.

Lester, A. and Bindman, G. (1972) *Race and Law*. Harmondsworth, Penguin.

Levy, D. (1986) Here be witches! 'Anti-racism' and the making of a new inquisition. In F. Palmer (ed.), *Anti-Racism – An Assault on Education and Value*. London, Sherwood Press.

Lewis, R. (1988) *Anti-Racism: A Mania Exposed*. London, Quartet Books.

Liazos, A. (1972) The poverty of the sociology of deviance: Nuts, sluts and perverts, *Social Problems*, 20, 103–20.

Lockwood, D. (1958) *The Blackcoated Worker: A Study in Class Consciousness*. London, Allen and Unwin.

London Strategic Policy Unit (1987) *Women's Equality Group Newsletter*, No. 3, April. London, LSP.

Loveland, I. (1988) Discretionary decision-making in housing benefit schemes: A case study, *Policy and Politics*, 16(2), 99–115.

Lukacs, G. (1971) *History and Class Consciousness: Studies in Marxist Dialectics*. London, Heinemann.

Lukes, S. (1980) Socialism and equality. In J. Sterba (ed.), *Justice: Alternative Political Perspectives*. Belmont, CA, Wadsworth.

Lundhal, M. and Wadensjo, E. (1984) *Unequal Treatment: A Study in Neo-classical Theory of Discrimination*. London, Croom Helm.

Luxemburg, R. (1900/1970) Reform or revolution? In M. Waters (ed.), *Rosa Luxemburg Speaks*. New York, Pathfinder Press.

Luxemburg, R. (1906/1970) The mass strike, the political party and the trade unions. In M. Waters (ed.), *Rosa Luxemburg Speaks*. New York, Pathfinder Press.

Macdonald, I., Bhavnani, R., Khan, L. and John, G. (1989) *Murder in the Playground: The Report of the Macdonald Inquiry into Racism and Racial Violence in Manchester Schools*. London, Longsight Press.

MacGregor, K. (1990) Equality groups warn polys on poor record. *The Times Higher Educational Supplement*, 4 May 1990.

Macy, M. (1988) New class dissent among socio-cultural specialists: The effects of occupational self-direction and location in the public sector, *Sociological Forum*, 3, 325–56.

Mallet, S. (1968) *The New Middle Class*. Paris, Sevil Editions.

Marx, K. and Engels, F. (1848) *The Communist Manifesto*. Harmondsworth, Pelican.

Mason, D. (1990) Competing concepts of 'fairness' and the formulation and implementation of equal opportunity policies. In W. Ball and J. Solomos (eds), *Race and Local Politics*. London, Macmillan.

Mattausch, J. (1989) *A Commitment to Campaign: A Sociological Study of CND*. Manchester, Manchester University Press.

May, T. (1993) *Social Research: Issues, Methods and Process*. Buckingham, Open University Press.

McCrudden, C. (1982) Institutional discrimination, *Oxford Journal of Legal Studies*, 2, 303–67.

McKee, L. and O'Brien, M. (1983) Interviewing men: Taking gender seriously. In E. Gamarnikow, D. Morgan, J. Purvis and D. Taylorson (eds), *The Public and the Private*. London, Heinemann.

Measor, L. (1985) Interviewing – a strategy in qualitative research. In R. Burgess (ed.), *Strategies in Educational Research: Qualitative Methods*. London, Falmer Press.

Media Research Group (1987) *Media Coverage of London Councils*. London, Goldsmith's College, University of London.

Meth, M. (1972) *Brothers of All Men*. London, Runnymede Trust Industrial Unit.

Mies, M. (1983) Towards a methodology for feminist research. In G. Bowles and R. Duelli Klien (eds), *Theories of Women's Studies*. London, Routledge and Kegan Paul.

Miles, R. (1982) *Racism and Migrant Labour*. London, Routledge and Kegan Paul.

Miles, R. (1989) *Racism*. London, Routledge.

Miles, R. and Phizacklea, A. (1977) *The TUC, Black Workers and New Commonwealth Immigration: 1954–1973*. Centre for Research in Ethnic Relations, University of Warwick.

Miles, R. and Phizacklea, A. (1978) The TUC and black workers: 1974–1976. *British Journal of Industrial Relations*, 16, 195–207.

Miles, R. and Phizacklea, A. (eds) (1979) *Racism and Political Action in Britain*. London, Routledge and Kegan Paul.

Miller, H. (1991) Academics and their labour process. In C. Smith, D. Knights and H. Willmott (eds), *White-Collar Work: The Non-Manual Labour Process*. London, Macmillan.

Mills, C.W. (1973) *The Sociological Imagination*. Harmondsworth, Penguin.

Mirza, H.S. (1994) Black women in higher education: Defining a space/finding a place. In L. Morley and V. Walsh (eds), *Feminist Academics: Creative Agents For Change*. London, Taylor and Francis.

Modood, T. (1992) *Not Easy Being British: Colour, Culture and Citizenship*. Stoke-on-Trent, Trentham Books.

Modood, T. (1993a) Subtle shades of distinction. *The Times Higher Educational Supplement*, 16 July 1993.

Modood, T. (1993b) The number of ethnic minority students in British higher education: some grounds for optimism, *Oxford Review of Education*, 19(2), 167–82.

Morgan, D. (1981) Men, masculinity and the process of sociological enquiry. In H. Roberts (ed.), *Doing Feminist Research*. London, Routledge.

Morgan, G. and Knights, D. (1991) Gendering jobs: Corporate strategy, managerial control and the dynamics of job segregation, *Work, Employment and Society*, 5(2), 181–200.

Morley, L. (1993) Glass ceiling or iron cage: Women in UK academia. Paper presented to the *Women's Studies Network Conference*, Nene College, Northampton.

Morris, J. (1991) *Pride Against Prejudice: Transforming Attitudes to Disability*. London, Women's Press.

Mullard, C. (1984) *Anti-Racist Education: The Three O's*. London, National Association for Multi-Racial Education.

Myers, K. (1990) Review of 'equal opportunities in the new ERA', *Education*, 5 October, p. 295.

Nanton, P. and Fitzgerald, M. (1990) Race policies in local government: Boundaries or thresholds. In W. Ball and J. Solomos (eds), *Race and Local Politics*. London, Macmillan.

NATFHE (1993) *Members Handbook*. London, NATFHE.

Neal, S. (1995a) A question of silence? Anti-racist policies in higher education: Two case studies. In M. Griffiths and B. Troyna (eds), *'Race', Culture and Anti-Racism*. Stoke-on-Trent, Trentham Books.

Neal, S. (1995b) Researching powerful people from a feminist and anti-racist perspective: A note on gender, marginality and collusion, *British Journal of Educational Research*, 21(4), 517–31.

Newman, J. (1959) *The Idea of a University*. London, Image Books.

Nixon, J. (1982) The Home Office and race relations policy: Co-ordinator or initiator?, *Journal of Public Policy*, 2(4), 365–78.

Nkweto Simmonds, F. (1997) My body, myself: How does a black woman do sociology? In H.S. Mirza (ed.), *Black British Feminism*. London, Routledge.

Nugent, N. and King, R. (1979a) Ethnic minorities, scapegoating and the extreme
right. In R. Miles and A. Phizacklea (eds), *Racism and Political Action in Britain*.
London, Routledge and Kegan Paul.

Nugent, N. and King, R. (eds) (1979b) *Respectable Rebels*. London, Hodder and
Stoughton.

Oakley, A. (1981) Interviewing women: A contradiction in terms? In H. Roberts
(ed.), *Doing Feminist Research*. London, Routledge.

Offe, C. (1984) *Contradictions of the Welfare State*. London, Hutchinson.

Opie, A. (1992) Qualitative research, appropriation of the 'other' and empowerment, *Feminist Review*, 40, 52–69.

Ouseley, H. (1984) Local authority race initiatives. In C. Boddy and M. Fudge (eds),
Local Socialism. London, Macmillan.

Ouseley, H. (1990) Resisting institutional change. In W. Ball and J. Solomos (eds),
Race and Local Politics. London, Macmillan.

Ozga, J. (1990) Policy research and policy theory: A comment on Fitz and Halpin,
Journal of Education Policy, 5(4), 359–62.

Palmer, F. (1986) *Anti-Racism: An Assault on Education and Value*. London, Sherwood
Press.

Parkin, F. (1968) *Middle Class Radicalism: The Social Bases of the British Campaign for
Nuclear Disarmament*. Manchester, Manchester University Press.

Parmar, P. (1981) Young Asian women: A critique of the pathological approach,
Multiracial Education, 9(3), 19–29.

Phizacklea, A. and Miles, R. (1980) *Labour and Racism*. London, Routledge and
Kegan Paul.

Phizacklea, A. and Miles, R. (1987) The British trade union movement and racism.
In G. Lee and R. Loveridge (eds), *The Manufacture of Disadvantage*. Milton Keynes,
Open University Press.

Phizacklea, A. and Miles, R. (1992) The British Trade Union movement and racism.
In P. Braham, A. Rattansi and R. Skellington (eds), *Racism and Antiracism:
Inequalities, Opportunities and Policies*. London, Sage in association with Open
University Press.

Prandy, K. (1965) *Professional Employees*. London, Faber.

Prandy, K., Stewart, A. and Blackburn, R. (1983) *White Collar Unionism*. London,
Macmillan.

Punch, M. (1986) *The Politics and Ethics of Fieldwork*. Beverly Hills, CA, Sage.

Radin, B. (1966) Coloured workers and British trade unions, *Race*, VII(2), 157–73.

Ramanzanoglu, C. (1987) Sex and violence in academic life or you can't keep a
good woman down. In J. Hanmer and M. Maynard (eds), *Women, Violence and
Social Control*. London, Macmillan.

Ramanzanoglu, C. (1992) On feminist methodology: Male reason versus female
empowerment. *Sociology*, 26(2), 207–12.

Ramdin, R. (1987) *The Making of the Black Working Class in Britain*. Aldershot,
Gower.

Ratcliffe, P. (1990) Race and ethnicity research in Britain: Some ethical and political considerations. Paper presented to the *XIIth World Congress of Sociology*, Madrid,
July–August.

Rattansi, A. (1992) Changing the subject? Racism, culture and education. In
J. Donald and A. Rattansi (eds), *'Race', Culture and Difference*. London, Sage.

Rex, J. and Tomlinson, S. (1979) *Colonial Immigrants in a British City: A Class Analysis.* London, Routledge and Kegan Paul.

Robbins Report (1963) *Higher Education: Report of the Committee Appointed by the Prime Minister Under the Chairmanship of Lord Robbins 1961–63.* London, HMSO.

Roberts, K., Cook, F., Clark, S. and Semeonoff, E. (1977) *The Fragmentary Class Structure.* London, Heinemann.

Robinson, E. (1968) *The New Polytechnics: The People's Universities.* London, Cornmarket Press.

Rose, E. and Associates (1969) *Colour and Citizenship: A Report on British Race Relations.* Oxford, Oxford University Press.

Runnymede Trust (1971a) *Policy or Drift? How Three London Firms Handle Racial Integration in the Workforce.* London, Runnymede Trust Industrial Unit.

Runnymede Trust (1971b) *Some Typical Discrimination Complaints.* London, Runnymede Trust Industrial Unit.

Runnymede Trust (1974) Trade unions and immigrant workers, *New Community,* IV(1), 19–36.

Russell, P. (1993) *Academic Freedom.* London, Routledge.

Said, E. (1978) *Orientalism: Western Conceptions of the Orient.* London, Penguin.

Salter, B. and Tapper, T. (1994) *The State and Higher Education.* London, Woburn Press.

Saunders, P. (1984) Rethinking local politics. In M. Boddy and C. Fudge (eds), *Local Socialism.* London, Macmillan.

Scarman, Lord (1982) *The Brixton Disorders 10–12 April 1981: Report of the Inquiry by the Rt Hon. The Lord Scarman OBE.* London, HMSO.

Scruton, R., Ellis-Jones, A. and O'Keefe, D. (1985) *Education and Indoctrination: An Attempt at Definition and a Review of Social and Political Implications.* London, Educational Research Centre.

Simeone, A. (1987) *Academic Women: Working Towards Equality.* London, Bergin and Garcey.

Sivanandan, A. (1973) Editorial, *Race Today,* August.

Sivanandan, A. (1982) *A Different Hunger.* London, Pluto.

Skellington, R. (1996) *'Race' in Britain Today* (2nd edn). London, Sage in association with Open University Press.

Small, S. (1994) *Racialised Barriers: The Black Experience in the United States and England in the 1980s.* London, Routledge.

Smart, C. (1984) *The Ties That Bind: Law, Marriage and the Reproduction of Patriarchal Relations.* London, Routledge and Kegan Paul.

Smith, D. (1977) *Racial Disadvantage in Britain.* Harmondsworth, Penguin.

Snow, D. and Anderson, L. (1993) *Down on Their Luck: A Study of Homeless People.* Los Angeles, CA, University of California Press.

Solomos, J. (1983) *The Politics of Black Youth Unemployment.* Working Papers on Ethnic Relations No. 20. Birmingham, Research Unit on Ethnic Relations, Aston University.

Solomos, J. (1988) *Black Youth, Racism and the State.* Cambridge, Cambridge University Press.

Solomos, J. (1989) *Race Relations Research and Social Policy: A Review of Some Recent Debates and Controversies.* Policy Papers in Ethnic Relations No. 18. Coventry, CRER, University of Warwick.

Solomos, J. (1993) *Race and Racism in Britain.* London, Macmillan.

Solomos, J. and Back, L. (1995) *Race, Politics and Social Change.* London, Routledge.

Solomos, J. and Ball, W. (1990) New initiatives and the possibilities of reform. In W. Ball and J. Solomos (eds), *Race and Local Politics.* London, Macmillan.

Spender, D. (1980) *Man Made Language.* London, Routledge and Kegan Paul.

Spender, D. (1984) The gatekeepers: A feminist critique of academic publishing. In H. Roberts (ed.), *Doing Feminist Research.* London, Routledge and Kegan Paul.

Spender, D. (1987) *The Education Papers: Women's Quest for Equality in Britain, 1850–1912.* London, Routledge and Kegan Paul.

Stacey, J. (1988) Can there be a feminist ethnography?, *Women's Studies International Forum,* 11(1), 21–7.

Stanfield, J. (ed.) (1993) *A History of Race Relations Research: First Generation Recollections.* London, Sage.

Stanfield, J. and Dennis, R. (eds) (1993) *Race and Ethnicity in Research Methods.* London, Sage.

Stanley, L. (1991) Feminist auto/biography and feminist epistemology. In J. Aaron and S. Walby (eds), *Out of the Margins: Women's Studies in the Nineties.* London, Falmer Press.

Stanley, L. and Wise, S. (1983a) 'Back into the personal' or: Our attempt to construct 'feminist research'. In G. Bowles and R. Duelli Klien (eds), *Theories of Women's Studies.* London, Routledge and Kegan Paul.

Stanley, L. and Wise, S. (1983b) *Breaking Out: Feminist Consciousness and Feminist Research.* London, Routledge and Kegan Paul.

Stenhouse, L. (1982) The conduct, analysis and reporting of case study in educational research and evaluation. In R. McCormick (ed.), *Calling Education to Account.* London, Heinemann.

Stuart Mill, J. (1869/1963) Inaugural Address at St Andrews University. In A.W. Levi (ed.), *The Six Great Humanistic Essays of John Stuart Mill.* New York, Washington Square Press.

Tapper, T. and Salter, B. (1978) *Education and the Political Order.* London, Macmillan.

Taylor, P. (1992) *Ethnic Group Data for University Entry.* Project Report for CVCP Working Group on Ethnic Data. Coventry, CRER, University of Warwick.

Tizard, B. and Pheonix, A. (1993) *Black, White or Mixed Race: Race and Racism in the Lives of Young People of Mixed Parentage.* London, Routledge.

Trade Union Congress (1981) *TUC Charter for Equality of Opportunity for Black Workers.* London, TUC.

Trade Union Congress (1990) *Union Rules Against Racism: Guidance Notes for Unions.* London, TUC.

Trade Union Congress (1992) *Involvement of Black Workers in Trade Unions.* London, TUC.

Trotsky, L. (1929/1975) The errors in principle of syndicalism. In *Leon Trotsky on the Trade Unions.* New York: Pathfinder (pamphlet).

Troyna, B. (1984) Fact or artefact? The 'educational underachievement' of black pupils, *British Journal of Sociology of Education,* 5(2), 153–66.

Troyna, B. (1993) Sounding a discordant note? 'Being critical' and 'critical beings' in education policy research. Paper presented to the *Fifth Cambridge International Conference on Educational Evaluation,* University of Cambridge, December.

Troyna, B. and Carrington, R. (1989) Whose side are we on? Ethical dilemmas in research on 'race' and education. In R. Burgess (ed.), *The Ethics of Educational Research.* Lewes, Falmer Press.

Troyna, B. and Carrington, B. (1990) *Education, Racism and Reform.* London, Routledge.

Troyna, B. and Williams, J. (1986) *Racism, Education and the State*. London, Croom Helm.

Universities Central Clearing and Admissions (1991–92) *Statistical Supplement to 13th Report*. London, UCCA.

Vincent, C. (1993) Community participation? The establishment of 'City's' Parents' Centre, *British Educational Research Journal*, 19(3), 227–42.

Virdee, S. and Grint, K. (1994) Black self-organization in trade unions, *Sociological Review*, 42(2), 202–226.

Walker, R. (1980) The conduct of educational case studies: Ethics, theory and procedures. In W. Dockrell and D. Hamilton (eds), *Rethinking Educational Research*. London, Hodder and Stoughton.

Wallsgrove, R. (1980) *The Masculine Face of Science*. Brighton, Women and Science Group.

Ware, V. (1992) *Beyond the Pale: White Women, Racism and History*. London, Verso.

Weiner, G. (1992) Staffing policies in further and higher education: Setting the scene. Paper presented at the *Equal Opportunities in Management Symposium, CEDAR International Conference*, University of Warwick, Coventry, May.

Weir, D. (1976) Radical managerialism: Middle managers' perceptions of collective bargaining, *British Journal of Industrial Relations*, XIV, 324–38.

Wilkins, R. (1993) Taking it personally: A note on emotion and autobiography, *Sociology*, 27(1), 93–100.

Williams, G., Blackstone, T. and Metcalf, D. (1974) *The Academic Labour Market: Economic and Social Aspects*. London, Elsevier.

Williams, J., Cocking, J. and Davies, L. (1989) *Words or Deeds: A Review of Equal Opportunity Policies in Higher Education*. London, CRE.

Williams, P. (1992) *The Alchemy of Race and Rights*. London, Virago.

Wilson, E. (1985) *Adorned in Dreams*. London, Virago.

Wilson, E. (1989) *Through the Looking Glass: A History of Dress from 1860 to the Present Day*. London, BBC Books.

Wrench, J. (1986) *Unequal Comrades: Trade Unions, Equal Opportunity and Racism*. CRER, Policy Papers in Ethnic Relations no. 5, University of Warwick.

Wrench, J. (1992) Ethnic minorities and workplace organisation in Britain: Trade unions, participation and racism. Paper presented at the *Conference on Ethnic Minorities and Their Chances of Participation: A Comparison Between France, Britain, the Netherlands and Federal Republic of Germany*, Bonn, December.

Wright, E. (1978) *Class, Crisis and the State*. London, New Left Books.

Wright, E. (1979) Intellectuals and the class structure of capitalist society. In P. Walker (ed.), *Between Labour and Capital*. Hassocks, Sussex: Harvester Press.

Young, I. (1990) *Justice and the Politics of Difference*. Princeton, NJ, Princeton University Press.

Young, K. (1989) The space between words: Local authorities and the concept of equal opportunities. In R. Jenkins and J. Solomos (eds), *Racism and Equal Opportunity Policies in the 1980s*. Cambridge, Cambridge University Press.

Young, K. (1992) Approaches to policy development in the field of equal opportunities. In P. Braham, A. Rattansi and R. Skellington (eds), *Racism and Antiracism: Inequalities, Opportunities and Policies*. London, Sage.

Young, K. and Connelly, N. (1981) *Policy and Practice in the Multi-Racial City*. London, Policy Studies Institute.

Index

The Society for Research into Higher Education

The Society for Research into Higher Education exists to stimulate and coordinate research into all aspects of higher education. It aims to improve the quality of higher education through the encouragement of debate and publciation on issues of policy, on the organization and management of higher education institutions, and on the curriculum and teaching methods.

The Society's income is derived from subscriptions, sales of its books and journals, conference fees and grants. It receives no subsidies, and is wholly independent. Its individual members include teachers, researches, managers and students. Its corporate members are institutions of higher education, research institutes, professional, industrial and governmental bodies. Members are not only from the UK, but from elsewhere in Europe, from America, Canada and Australasia, and it regards its international work as among its most important activities.

Under the imprint *SRHE & Open University Press*, the Society is a specialist publisher of research, having some 60 titles in print. The Editorial Board of the Society's Imprint seeks authoritative research or study in the above fields. It offers competitive royalties, a highly recognizable format in both hardback and paperback and the worldwide reputation of the Open University Press.

The Society also publishes *Studies in Higher Education* (three times a year), which is mainly concerned with academic issues, *Higher Education Quarterly* (formerly *Universities Quarterly*), mainly concerned with policy issues, *Research into Higher Education Abstracts* (three times a year), and *SRHE News* (four times a year).

The Society holds a major annual conference in December, jointly with an institution of higher education. In 1994 the topic was 'The Student Experience' at the University of York. In 1995 it was 'The Changing University' at Heriot-Watt University in Edinburgh and in 1996, 'Working in Higher Education' at Cardiff Institute of Higher Education. Conferences in 1997 include 'Beyond the First Degree' at the University of Warwick.

The Society's committees, study groups and branches are run by the members. The groups at present include:

Teacher Education Study Group
Continuing Education Group
Staff Development Group
Excellence in Teaching and Learning

Benefits to members

Individual

Individual members receive:

- *SRHE News*, the Society's publications list, conference details and other material included in mailings.
- Greatly reduced rates for *Studies in Higher Education* and *Higher Education Quarterly*.
- A 35 per cent discount on all SRHE & Open University Press publications.
- Free copies of the Proceedings – commissioned papers on the theme of the Annual Conference.
- Free copies of *Research into Higher Education Abstracts*.
- Reduced rates for conferences.
- Extensive contacts and scope for facilitating initiatives.
- Reduced reciprocal memberships.
- Free copies of the *Register of Members' Research Interests*.

Corporate

Corporate members receive:

- All benefits of individual members, plus.
- Free copies of *Studies in Higher Education*.
- Unlimited copies of the Society's publications at reduced rates.
- Special rates for its members e.g. to the Annual Conference.
- The right to submit application for the Society's research grants.

Membership details: SRHE, 3 Devonshire Street, London W1N 2BA, UK. Tel: 0171 637 2766. Fax: 0171 637 2781. email: srhe@MAILBOX.ulcc.ac.uk
World Wide Web: http://www.srhe.ac.uk./srhe/
Catalogue: SRHE & Open University Press, Celtic Court, 22 Ballmoor, Buckingham MK18 1XW. Tel: 01280 823388. Fax: 01280 823233. email: enquiries@openup.co.uk

EQUAL OPPORTUNITIES IN COLLEGES AND UNIVERSITIES
TOWARDS BETTER PRACTICES

Maureen Farish, Joanna McPake, Janet Powney and Gaby Weiner

This book is the *first* attempt to consider the effectiveness of equal opportunities policies for staff (in colleges and universities) after the policies have been passed and implemented. It suggests future strategies for policy-makers and equal opportunities 'activists' in the light of the findings which concern structure, policy coherence and policy contradiction.

It provides an account, through the detailed case-studies of three educational institutions (one further education college, one 'new' and one 'old' university) of how equal opportunities policy-making has developed over the last decade and what gains have been made. It also examines the complexity of trying to judge the effectiveness of such policies by viewing policy from a number of standpoints including those of managers and policy-makers, those charged with implementing the policies (for instance, equal opportunities or women's officers), and those at the receiving end. In trying to unravel the complexity, what emerges is the importance of institutional history and context as well as policy structure and content.

Contents
Setting the context of equal opportunities in educational organizations – Borough college incorporated: case study – Town university: case study – Metropolitan university: case study – Critical moments and illuminative insights – Codifying policy and practice – Contrasting contexts – Shared themes – Munro bagging: towards better practices – Apendix: research methodology – Bibliography – Index.

224pp   0 335 19416 8 (Paperback)   0 335 19417 6 (Hardback)

RACE FOR A CHANGE IN CONTINUING AND HIGHER EDUCATION

Mal Leicester

Mal Leicester argues that an antiracist, pluralist approach can transform adult education in higher education and in other contexts; that adult and continuing education departments are potential agents of change in higher education with regard to the development of anti-racist higher education; and that race and culture issues, properly understood, could empower higher education in its most central tasks. She justifies these claims by focusing on both theoretical debates and practical experience (drawing on her own and others' empirical research).

Race for a Change in Continuing and Higher Education will stimulate thinking on theoretical considerations, and offers guidance for practice both in terms of student learning and of securing relevant institutional change.

Contents
Part 1: Antiracist continuing education: agent and model – Continuing education as change agent: inreach and outreach – Conceptual clarification: 'racism' and 'antiracist education' – Conceptual clarification: 'antiracist continuing education' – Practising what we preach: departmental change – Change agents and models: a UCACE survey revisited – Part 2: Continuing antiracist education: the university transformed – Coming of age: the mature university – Outreach: antiracist access – Access and maintaining academic standards – Inreach: accessibility and the antiracist university – Higher education for all – Appendix – Bibliography – Index.

160pp   0 335 09767 7 (Paperback)   0 335 09768 5 (Hardback)

ACADEMIC WOMEN

Ann Brooks

Dr Brooks is able to document the structural basis of power, patronage and prejudice . . . should be read and valued by a wide audience.

Ann Oakley

- How and why have women academics experienced patterns of exclusion, segregation and discrimination in higher education?
- To what extent are academic relationships characterized by endemic sexism in defence of male privilege?
- What parallels are there in patterns of discrimination and disadvantage for academic women in different cultural contexts?

Academic Women explores these questions and investigates the relationships between gender, power and the academy through an analysis of the position of academic women in higher education in the UK and New Zealand. It considers the gap between the models of equality and academic fairness which are said to characterize academic life and the sexist reality of the academy. Ann Brooks combines new and original data drawn from statistical evidence and from the resuits of questionnaires and interviews with British and New Zealand women academics; and this evidence is located within a wider framework of historical evidence on the position of academic women in both countries.

Contents
Foreword – Introduction – Jobs for the boys: academic women in the UK, 1900–1900 – Women's experience of the UK academy – Academic women in Aotearoa/New Zealand, 1970– 1990 – Academic women's experience of the academy in Aotearoa/New Zealand – Gender, power and the academy: patterns of discrimination and disadvantage for academic women in the UK and Aotearoa/New Zealand – Conclusion – Appendix 1: Researching the academic community – Methodological issues – Appendix 2: Questionnaire – Researching the experience of women academics in higher education – Appendix 3: Massey University – Academic salaries – Notes – Bibliography – Index.

192pp   0 335 19599 7 (Paperback)   0 335 19600 4 (Hardback)